Anais, Art and Artists

Something was coming

C coughed C coughed

which held it

and yanked it out. C went back to bed and

this book in begin to thread the of broke c. am me

was coming to

said and C have just got this morning C Ok took out

something startling was

throat of my

Ok took out Cy

There is an instrument called the quena made of human bones. Owes its origin to the worship of an ancestor for his mistress. When she died he made a flute out of her bones. The quena has a more penetrating, more haunting sound than the ordinary flute.

Those who write know the process. I thought of it as I was spitting out my heart.

Only I do not wait for my love to die. The quena is made only of human bones.

from
Anaïs Nin's
House of Incest

calligram by
Georgiana Peacher

Anais, Art and Artists,

a Collection of Essays

edited by

Sharon Spencer

The Penkevill Publishing Company
Greenwood, Florida

Copyright © 1986
Sharon Spencer

ISBN 0–913283–11–8

Printed in the United States of America

CONTENTS

Preface

It was my great privilege to be among the many men and women whom Anais Nin welcomed as spiritual children. I was introduced to her by Anna Balakian, who directed my graduate study in Comparative Literature at New York University. Anais Nin's impact on my life was immediate, intense, and, seemingly, permanent. When Harper & Row was considering publishing my first novel, Anais said, "Use me. Use my name now while I am known to the general public. Tell them I will provide an introduction." I did this, and Anais donated her own keenly sensitive reading of The Space Between to the book.

A year or so later, Anna Balakian said to me: "You should write a book about Anais Nin's works." I had already thought of doing this and I was extremely pleased that my loved and respected mentor considered it a good idea too. The result was my interpretive study, Collage of Dreams, first published, so appropriately, by The Swallow Press, and reissued in 1983 in an expanded paperback version by Harcourt, Brace, Jovanovich. Anais saw the manuscript but unfortunately she died before it was published. Because the chapter titled "The Art of Ragpicking" amused and pleased her, I have chosen to reprint it in this collection. The energy of my project was focused on putting Anais's work, especially her fiction, in the context of modernism and feminism and to show its relationships to psychology and to the other arts. Anais's fiction is radiant work, radical in many ways and deeply reverent. Anais wanted it to be experienced directly by the senses, absorbed, not "understood" cerebrally, with detachment. It is truly the "novel of the future" and will perhaps always remain light years distant from acceptance based on the conventional expectations of the literary establishment. Anais's novels will be waiting for the readers of the future, a treasury of resplendent brilliantly colored images wrought to lure them into the unsuspected depths of the inner life.

During the last two years of Anais's life I visited her several times in California. I had never before had to witness the process of death from cancer, and before my first visit I was afraid I would break down in her presence. "You won't," one of Anais's West Coast "daughters" assured me. "Anais is in control of the mood. She sets the tone. What we have to do is wear our brightest, most exotic clothes and sing and dance for her."

And that is what we did. The style with which Anais confronted agonizing pain was, predictably, both elegant and courageous. As intense as her suffering was, she clung to life so tenaciously that her suffering was prolonged. Those who loved her, perhaps especially her companion Rupert Pole, who cared for her during this time with staggering energy and cheerfulness, greeted her eventual death with sorrow lightened by relief.

Near the time of Anais's death, I dreamed of her (she appeared in many of my most significant dreams). Anais was floating gracefully in the atmosphere wearing one of her simple Indian cotton dresses and I was attached to her by a very long elastic cord. I was here and she was there. The marvelous thing was that the cord was infintely elastic.

Among the many gifts Anais gave me were contacts with people she knew, truly extraordinary people, all in one way or another, creative. The list is long: Ian Hugo (Hugh Guiler), Anais's brother, Joaquin Nin-Culmell, her friend Frank Alberti, and John Ferrone, her editor at Harcourt Brace Jovanovich, Bettina L. Knapp, whose friendship with Anais started with their shared enthusiasm for Antonin Artaud, and Stephen Goode, who, as editor of *Studies in the Twentieth Century*, had provided welcome for numerous articles about Anais's writings. Now the founder of the Penkevill Publishing Company, Stephen Goode recently invited Bettina Knapp to be the general editor of a series of annuals devoted to modern literature. *Anais, Art and Artists* is the second work in this series, and it brings to fruition the dream that Bettina and I have shared for several years of creating a collection of essays to celebrate the spirit of Anais's life and work. It was originality, above all, that intrigued her and attracted her to other people. "A woman artist makes her own patterns," Anais wrote in *Collages*, attributing this boldness to the painter Renate (in life, Renate Druks whose words provide the closing celebratory note of this collection). All the authors and artists whose work appears here are personal friends or acquaintances. Most of them knew Anais, some quite well. All have something unique to say about Anais, art and artists, and all are among the "sensitive Americans" to whom Anais dedicated *The Novel of the Future* with the invocation that they might "create a sensitive America."

It is in this spirit that I have brought together the varied pieces that comprise *Anais, Art and Artists.*

Sharon Spencer
Summer, 1986

Photograph by Deigh Navin in celebration of U. S. publication of *Under a Glass Bell*. The background displays the original copper plates of Ian Hugo. Photgraph is reprinted with the permission of Ian Hugo.

Letter from Anais

by Jamake Highwater

When word came from Los Angeles on January 14 that Anais Nin was gone, I angrily pushed aside the frantic work of the future and solemnly turned to a precious folio of letters from the past. Among them were the words of an exuberant and gentle woman who had befriended me almost from the first day I had decided to be a writer. To me, and to many other writers, Anais Nin became a voice of unfailing concern, unrepressed enthusiasm and — yes — *undying* affection.

Anais had a sense about people. She instantly knew which of us could be counted upon to fight it out to the bitter end. Fortunately she detected my tenacity and I became one of the lucky ones who received her encouragement, criticism, and advice.

"Don't let what happens to me discourage you," she scribbled on a sheet of *In Flight American Airlines* stationery, as she hovered over the American landscape enroute to New York. "I have many handicaps you don't have. I'm a woman, and I have been 'typed' as avant-garde. My case as a writer is individual. You may have a much easier time. But I would advise you to go to New York. It is easier for a writer there. New York is a writer's city. You could meet an agent, magazine people, etc. Don't lose courage. I haven't! *Anais*."

I was a terribly misplaced American Indian kid trailing after my father, who was an alcoholic stuntman in western movies. We annually made our long trail of tears from Montana to Hollywood where papa could make some money and drink most of it up on the way back home. I had decided that I wanted to be a writer despite the fact that my people for centuries had possessed not a written but an oral tradition and had produced very few writers. Anais Nin read what I have written and decided that I might have whatever it is that makes a writer. She got to know me through James Leo Herlihy, who worked in those days at a little book shop in Hollywood where I spent every day among the stacks of old books and ragged literary magazines. Jim and Anais took me in as a fellow-writer despite my western garb, my tangled long hair, and my youth — at the time I was 12 years old, claiming eighteen with the help of an unsuccessful moustache. I was already six feet tall, prematurely rebellious, and precociously crammed with James Joyce, T. S. Eliot, and overflowing with arrogant pride in my Indian heritage. I adored Virginia Woolf, Geronimo, and Anais Nin.

Then in February, 1954, Anais left for New York and I told Jim Herlihy that I didn't think I could survive without her. Jim was older and he had just published his first short story (*Laughter in the Grave-yard.*) But I was still a kid with three huge unpublished novels and a stack of short stories. I spilled out my sense of melodrama in a long letter to Anais. I was a child and I did not realize that at the time she was ill and worried and very busy. But she put aside whatever she was doing and wrote a letter to me which has always been an emblem of courage and a source of encouragement.

On the day I learned that Anais was gone I unfolded the two pages of that precious old letter and found in the words a perfect portrait of the Anais Nin whose friendship helped me get from aspiring misfit to successful author.

"Why one writes is a question I can answer easily, having asked it so often of myself. I believe one writes because one has to create a world in which one can live. I could not live in any of the worlds offered to me: the world of my parents, or American life in general, or the world of wars, or any of my lovers' worlds. I had to create a world of my own, like a climate, a country, an atmosphere in which I could breathe, reign, and re-create myself when destroyed by living. That, I believe, is the reason for every work of art. The artist is the only one who knows the world is a subjective creation, that there is a choice to be made, a selection of the elements one will live and love with. It is a materialization, an incarnation of our inner world. Then we hope to attract others into it, to impose this particular vision and to share it with others. When the second stage is not reached, the brave artist continues nevertheless. The others — you and me — occasionally lose heart. But the *few moments* of communication with the world, with others, is worth the pain, for when it is achieved it is in terms of your true self.

"Now there are easier ways to communicate, directly through human relationships, but it is not the same; it is not in terms of our inner reality, on our own terms, by way of our own language. We also write to make our life heightened, bearable, and more infinite. We write to lure and enchant our lovers. We write to serenade them. We write to taste life twice, in the moment and in retrospection. We write, like Proust, to render all of it eternal and to persuade ourselves that we are eternal. We write to be able to speak, to be able to explore all our secret and hidden selves, or we write like Genet to rebel against the world, and to destroy it, or we write like Henry Miller to throw bombs at it, or we write to make a larger world, as I often do, when I feel strangled by the pettiness, or the constrictions, restrictions, taboos, lies, falseties . . . .

"Shall I go on? . . . . or have I said enough to encourage you? But I only want to encourage you if it means that much to you, if you breathe through writing, cry out through writing. Otherwise, don't write. It is ill-paid; it is non-commercial, and it is completely off beat with the trend of the times, which is supplanting the image and as far as writing goes, going the way of barbarian epochs . . . back to non-speech, primitive images, etc. Well, America is primitive. It hasn't much use for language. But if you write for the reasons I suggest, then you have to do it. When I don't I feel my world is shrinking. I feel I am in a prison. I feel I lose my fire, my life, and my color . . . Writing should be a necessity as the sea needs to heave. I call it breathing."

Now the breathing has stopped.

But the writing of Anais Nin will sustain her fire, her life, and her color. I was never as happy for anybody as when fame finally came to Anais. She desperately wanted it and she was ideally suited for it. Then almost at once, as if her long siege would not be rewarded, a new battle began against cancer. "But the few moments of communication with the world, with others, is worth the pain," she wrote to me long ago. Her few moments are over. Now the pain of her loss goes on.

"Anais Nin Observed," from the film of the same title by director Robert Snyder, released in 1973. This photograph is reproduced with the permission of the Anais Foundation in Los Angeles, California.

The Birth of a Vocation
by Marie-Claire Van der Elst

"It was our arrival in New York with wicker trunks, birdcages, a violin case, and no money. Aunts and uncles and cousins on the docks. Negro porters who throw themselves on our belongings. I was obstinately holding on to my brother's violin case. *I wanted people to know I was an artist.*"

The Diary of Anais Nin: 1927-1931

The scene described here took place in August, 1914, and is remembered, supposedly, in 1933, so that between the precise time of the event — when Anais was a child — and the uncertain time of the narration — when she was a full-fledged writer — some twenty years have elapsed. Possibly even fifty; the first volume of the *Diary* was not published until 1966 and we do not know to what extent the published version, especially in its many reminiscences, follows the original notebooks for the corresponding years. Whatever the case may be, and even though the same scene is depicted somewhat differently in the first volume of *The Early Diary: Linotte* where no mention is made of the violin case, there is no reason to doubt the truth of that statement; already at the age of eleven not only did Anais Nin consider herself an artist, but she also wanted to be recognized as such. Here, let us open a parenthesis to point out that if the scene remembered is more vivid, more pregnant than the one written soon after the event, this is not due simply to the fact that the mature woman had developed the talent of the child, it is due largely to emotional distance which enables the artist to reach the quintessence, which is what art is all about according to Anais Nin.

The question we would like to tackle now is this one: how far is it possible to trace the birth of Anais Nin's vocation? How did it originate? We know it was an early vocation, and this is confirmed by her in an interview which was conducted by her friend Daisy Aldan in 1969 just after the publication of the third volume of the *Diary*: "As far back as I remember, I knew I was going to be a writer. Very early it became an *idée fixe*." This statement does not, however, throw any light on the how and why of her vocation, and this is what we want to examine now.

One fact imposes itself at once; it is through music that Anais was initiated into the world of art. In this her father's influence was determining; without the first-hand experience of music during her childhood, Anais Nin would never have become the writer she was. Her earliest recollections are of "Much music, quartets, quintets, singing. My father played with Pablo Casals. . . .I used to fall asleep listening to chamber music" (*The Diary: 1927-1933*, p. 217). From the outset she was steeped in music, and it left a permanent imprint upon her. Music meant harmony, as opposed to the cacophony in everyday life resulting from the quarrels between her parents, quarrels which eventually led to their separation. All through her life Anais Nin was to retain this notion that one function of art is to provide an escape from a painful life, an antidote to frustrations and anxieties. The artist substitutes his dream for reality, which he transmutes through his own alchemy. So when she suffered, when she longed for an impossible reconciliation between her parents, instinctively she turned to writing for comfort — she also turned to religion, but this we will discuss later. Thus, she wrote in order to forget, to create another world where she could feel secure and at peace. In the interview just mentioned, with Daisy Aldan, Anais said: "I began to write at the age of nine, when I was told I would never walk again", that is, at the time of her appendicitis in Brussels, only a few months before her father abandoned his family in Arcachon. In other words, two concomitant disasters, a doctor's wrong diagnosis but, chiefly, her father's desertion, acted as catalysts in the process that formed her literary vocation.

We must not think that with Joaquin Nin's departure music also left. In fact, Anais was never cut off from music; to begin with, her mother was a singer, and her two brothers were musicians, one a violinist and the other a pianist. When they came to New York, there were many (often Cuban and Spanish) musicians among their friends, especially in the brownstone house where Mrs. Nin rented rooms. Anais herself took piano lessons for awhile, but does not seem to have enjoyed playing, and she finally gave it up. However, she took up Spanish dancing. First in New York, then in Paris during the twenties with Antonio Francisco Miralles, Anais Nin acquired enough technique to become, had she wished, a professional dancer. This was not to be, but it is interesting to find that, before she succeeded as an American writer, she was attracted to Spanish dancing; even if indirectly, this was her father's legacy. Before she became an American artist (she liked to think of herself as an international or a cosmopolitan artist), she had written in French and had studied Spanish dancing.

It was to counterbalance the life in New York which she found it so hard to adjust to that she sought refuge in her diary which she kept in French long after she had mastered English. By this time it had become evident that the diary had ceased to be what it purported to be — a letter to her father. Curiously, only a few years after she had given up writing in French (she could always read it, and she spoke it without any accent), she returned to France with her husband and pursued her creative writing in English.

It is hardly an oversimplification to say that practically until 1940 Anais Nin used one language for everyday life and another for her writing; in America she wrote in French and in France she wrote in English. Paradoxical though this may seem, in fact it is quite in keeping with her attitude towards art. "I was always obsessed with transforming, with creating a world of my own. . ." (interview with Daisy Aldan). The differences between the language she spoke and the language she wrote only heightened the contrast between her art and her life.

Duane Schneider, who also interviewed Anais in 1969, questioned her about her relationship to her diary during the 40s, 50s, and 60s, as opposed to the 30s. She gave this answer: "I think the relationship to the diary changed. In the early diaries there is a distinct feeling of the ivory tower, the escape, the place where I could be truthful. And later on it changed in character. It became the diary of other people. . .". Beginning in 1940 when she returned to the United States, Anais approached writing differently. This was a turning point marked by the outbreak of the war. In fact, Anaïs and her husband left Paris because they had no choice, but their plan was to return as soon as the war was over; however, although they did not suspect it, they were back in the United States for good. Eventually, Anaïs's attitude towards English seems to have undergone a natural evolution. She discarded French, for which she had no real use, and came to consider English as the language that could best serve her both in art and everyday life. Even her correspondence with her mother was no longer in French; this is probably the best proof we have that Anaïs had fully reconciled herself to the idea that there was nothing wrong with writing in the language everyone around her spoke.

So far we have seen that Anaïs, who was a sensitive child with good reasons to feel unhappy, looked to art for a possible shelter; but for awhile religion also provided a haven from a disappointing life. We should now probe another question: what links exist, at the beginning of Anaïs's literary vocation, between religion and art, and why were they gradually dissociated, to the point that she gave up the one completely while persevering in the other?

Indeed, at an early stage, art and religion played similar roles for Anaïs: they enabled her to dream of an ideal life in which virtue was rewarded and all tears dried quickly. Her first attempts at poetry are little pieces which contain a good dose of religion, the kind of religion she had been indoctrinated with and which, for a time, she accepted whole-heartedly. I open the first volume of *Linotte: The Early Diary (1914-1920)* at random and on page 107 I read:

> Close your eyes to ugly things
> Open them to heaven's song.
> Close your eyes to false lights and things
> Open them to heaven's light so true . . .

and again on page 122:

> May is here; let us be full of joy.
> Oh! Tender mother, bless your children

> In this month honored by our song.
> Hosanna! for the Son of the Virgin Mary . . .

There is no doubt that to the thirteen-year-old author of these lines religion was a source of inspiration. We are not suggesting that Anais was obsessed with religious sentiments, far from it; at the time she wrote these poems she was also keeping her diary which gives a lively account of what was going on around her. She was also inventing extraordinary stories to entertain her brothers. In short, her creativity had more than one outlet. The fact remains though, that she did write, when she was quite young, somewhat imitative poems stuffed with religious references. She was also fascinated by the character of Joan of Arc whom she celebrated not so much as a saint, but as "the sweet heroine . . . who incarnated the soul of courage" (*Linotte*, p. 102). Around the age of twelve or thirteen Anais's religious fervor was often confused with her patriotic zeal for the French. She would pray to God to protect innocent French victims and defeat the enemies of France. Yet, interestingly, this passionate child also had her moments of depression or disillusionment, as witnessed by these lines:

> Here lies I know not what
> For I was nothing,
> Leaning only on my faith,
> For even joy was not mine.
>
> *Linotte*, p. 103

This sober mood contrasts with her fits of indignation against the Germans and her moments of exaltation about the brave people of France which Anais mingled with her prayers on their behalf. However, as she grew older and the war ended, making her patriotism irrelevant, Anais became more skeptical.

Before she was fifteen, she began to have her first doubts about religion in which, so it seems, she sought refuge and comfort. When Anais realized that her prayers were not granted, her fervor abated. Gradually, she became disillusioned with religion and turned away from it. In fact, her need for an emotional shelter had diminished, so it was natural that she should get rid of a religion which had lost all its attraction. Since it did not serve its purpose, it became cumbersome and meaningless.

With Anais's literary vocation, however, the evolution was the reverse. It had been growing steadily during all those years of childhood and adolescence when she was reading voraciously both in French and English. While she had no need for religion, literature, on the contrary, stimulated her own creativity. It provided an outlet for her imagination. Besides, her talent, which had always been appreciated and encouraged by her mother, began to be appreciated at school too. The period when Anais Nin dropped religion coincided with a new start in her literary vocation. English had displaced French: in 1920 she decided to write her diary in English, ostensibly because of her beloved cousin Eduardo who could not read French, but more probably because she was becoming estranged from her native country and by now felt at ease with English. Naturally, this was a slow process of maturation; she was still experimenting with her new language and exploring her own possibilities, her personal labyrinth. To Duane Schneider's questions about the "distinct stages of development" in her writing, referring to her first productions in English, Anais admitted: "It was a very awkward stage when I imitated everybody and couldn't find my own English. ... And then I began to say things in my own way." An artist was born.

The strange thing in the case of Anais Nin is not the precocity of her vocation, but that it should have taken so long for her to be recognized and published; the difficulties she had to overcome might have destroyed a writer with a less solid vocation. But she was both determined and disinterested, which is one reason nothing could defeat her. It would be a mistake, however, to believe that she had no encouragement, that she met only with hostility. Here is the other reason she persevered, undaunted; ever since she began to write, Anais always had around her people who shared her faith and wanted her to go on. First it was her mother, whose influence must probably be seen in Anais's "religious" poems, then it was her husband, Ian Hugo who financed the publication of her first books and also engraved the plates that illustrated the original editions of the novels. Anais's encounter with Henry Miller was also decisive because it opened new vistas to her talent. In short, Anais the writer was never alone, although she felt marginal. The small circle of her readers never stopped growing until she could rightly claim she was an international writer.

The Princess and the Frog: Anais Nin and Otto Rank
by Philip K. Jason

When Otto Rank took up residence in Paris in the spring of 1926, he had made many of his most important contributions to psychoanalytic literature. *The Trauma of Birth* was already being recognized as a classic work. Still, his career and reputation had fallen under the shadow of his split with Freud and the Viennese circle of which he had once been an important part. During his eight years in Paris, interspersed with lengthy stays in the United States, Rank embarked upon a second great period of creativity. He published extensively and saw many of his earlier works, often significantly revised, translated into French and English editions. He became a founder of the Psychological Center in Paris. Practicing under a Freudian ban, Rank made tremendous strides in his therapeutic technique, giving his patients a more active role and shortening their periods of treatment.[1]

Much of Rank's work, old and new, had to do with art and mythology. His explorations of the incest motif, the myths surrounding the births of legendary heroes, and the manifestations of doubles and Don Juan figures show one side of his fascination with folk and individual art. In the English language *Art and Artist* (1932), Rank's thinking on the artistic personality came to fruition. No one was better prepared, in the early 1930s, to treat the psychic woes of a myth-living and myth-generating artist-in-the-making than Otto Rank was. Perhaps, too, no one was more vulnerable to the spell of the artist than Rank, who saw himself, sometimes, as a sort of displaced artist.

In November of 1933 a delicately attractive woman of thirty arrived at the Paris office of Dr. Otto Rank. This woman, a budding writer who had already published a book on D. H. Lawrnece, was troubled by the conflicting demands of her roles as woman and artist and by a long-ingrained sense of paternal abandonment. When they met as patient and doctor, Anais Nin was already familiar with and greatly impressed by Rank's ideas. She had read his two most recent books: *Art and Artist* and the French volume of the same year that combined Rank's latest thoughts on the double and the Don Juan. Nin sought out Rank because she seemed to herself to be an incarnation of Rank's thinking; it was as if he had written about her. Rank, I believe, came to share the same notion. In this vital young artist, his concepts seemed to have taken on flesh.

For the rest of her life, Nin would testify to the enormous impact that Rank had upon her thinking, her writing, her very living. It was as if he was always with her. In terms of physical proximity and interaction, however, the relationship was relatively brief. For a year following their initial meeting, Nin was Rank's patient and student in Paris. In November of 1934, she followed him to New York in response to his pleas for assistance. There she worked with him and took on patients of her own under Rank's supervision until late spring of 1935 when she returned home. Nin visited New York again during the first four months of 1936, ostensibly to do more work with her patients. But there is almost no mention of Rank in the published diary for this period. In fact, there are no entries for February or March at all. A brief entry for April suggests that the relationship between them had become quite strained.[2] There were no further meetings. Rank died in 1939, some months before Nin's permanent move to the United States.

From the beginning of the relationship, Rank was bewitched. As the terms of the relationship changed, Dr. Rank, forty-nine when they first met, added to his role of psychoanalyst not only those of teacher, overseer, and colleague, but also that of frustrated lover. Certainly, in the latter stages of their relationship, Rank exhibited toward Nin a jealous, possessive love. Nin's selective comments in her published diary volumes, especially those at the beginning of the second volume which treat of the establishment of Rank's New York practice, suggest this pattern. The suggestion is confirmed by an autobiographical reading of Nin's story, "The Voice," first published in her 1939 volume *The Winter of Artifice*.[3] From Rank, unfortunately, we have no direct testimony.

Rank, it may be offered, served many of his own ends by assisting Nin with her difficulties. In the process of conducting her therapy,

Rank was brought close to the world of art and artists that Nin was building for herself. This freer, more spontaneous mode of living represented by Nin's friends and acquaintances was attractive to Rank; it was personally attractive, not just something to be studied. Moreover, in aiding Nin, Rank became vicariously engaged in the creative process, thus fulfilling an ambition of his own in an oblique way. Rank, the thwarted artist, could help the shaping of the diary and of Nin's early works-in-progress. Nin tells us that Rank "made" her finish *House of Incest,* helped her discover its meaning and proper conclusion, and insisted on saving certain key passages (II, 31).

Rank's proprietary interest in this work included his offer to publish it, and a preface he wrote for *House of Incest,* probably in 1935, is a further instance of Rank's serving his own needs through being in Nin's service.[4] The preface, primarily an examination of the Alraune (or Mandragora) legend, reads like an attempt by Rank to control — to possess — the work, rather than to introduce it. Here he can parade his erudition, ingratiate himself to Nin, be a man of letters, and send up a trial balloon toward the development of a viable feminine psychological construct. Rank's comments on Alraune — later named Sabina — parallel his comments on Lilith, the rebellious and mischievous "first woman" and alter-ego to Eve, whom he was to treat in detail in his late essay "Feminine Psychology and Masculine Ideology."[5]

In Nin's emotional problems and in her writings, Rank found the fundamental questions on the female psyche that he would continue to explore for the rest of the decade. Rank sensed the historical trap of a male-oriented culture, langauge, and philosophy. He was ready to admit that psychologists knew little about women. His relationship with Nin drove that point home, and it also challenged him to explore that situation. As Nin, with Rank's encouragement, continued to pursue her feminine approach to writing, that writing, along with their conversations, provided Rank with prods to his own thinking. While in a formal sense Nin was Rank's student, in another sense he was hers — he was a student of her behavior and her work. She exemplified an important problem that he strove to understand and resolve, a problem that was both professional and personal.

For Rank was in love with the person he was studying so closely. The living Anais Nin was all bound up in Rank's theories as well as his needs. In Rank's mind, Nin herself was sometimes an Alraune or Lilith: enticing but ungovernable. He strove to make her the more docile Eve (Djuna) by exercising control over her work, by calling her to assist him in New York, by asking her to commit time and energy to the task of translating his work on the incest motif. Rank was flattered by his relationship with Nin, and he was zealous to maintain it and control its terms.

The following passage from Nin's *Diary* (II, 38-39) suggests that Rank had more than a professional interest in Nin's behavior. The intensity and pattern of Rank's "discoveries" can be viewed as indications of an obsessive, possessive love:

> He would always ask me what I have been doing during the week. It was at this moment his magic would begin to operate, because no matter what I told him, from the most trivial: "I bought a bracelet," to the most important for me: "I found a job for my first patient," or "I wrote a page on minerals for *House of Incest*," Rank would immediately pounce on this fact with the joy of a discoverer, and raise this fragment to a brilliant, complete dazzling legend. The bracelet had a meaning, the minerals had a meaning, they revealed the amazing pattern by which I lived which only Rank could see completed and achieved. He would repeat over and over again: "You see, you see, you SEE." I had the feeling that I was doing extraordinary things. When I stopped before a window and bought a bracelet I expressed the drama of woman's dependence and enslavement. In this obscure little theatre of my unconscious, the denouement was this spontaneous purchase of a bracelet. According to Rank I was not seduced by the color and shape and texture of it, by my love of adornment. It was much more dramatic than that! Rank's interest was concentrated on unraveling the mystery of this ritual. "You see, you SEE." Not only the moment spent on Fifth Avenue was

revived, intensified, but all I had done during the week was like a perfect play, or a novel, fostered by Rank's revelation. I felt like an actress who had not known how moving her voice and gestures had been, their tremendous repercussion, but also like a creator preparing in some dim laboratory a life like a legend, and now reading the legend itself from an enormous book. And this was certainly part of the legend, Rank bowing over each incident, explaining, marveling at this miracle which had not seemed a miracle to me but a whim, my walking along and buying a bracelet, as miraculous to Rank as liquid turned to gold in an alchemist's bottle. The more I talked, the more stories I poured out, the more Rank convinced me that I had not only filled the world with a multitude of little acts but that all these acts were of deep significance and to be admired for the very act of their flowering. To please him, I would go back and find little actions I might have missed or lost down the dusty streets of my rich life, which, touched up by the illuminating wand of Rank's interpretation, acquired a new depth, a patina, a glow I had never noticed before, and which Rank feasted upon as if it were one of the most colorful tapestries he had ever seen. Colored lights played upon insignificant acts? Nothing was insignificant.

This is no mere description of a psychoanalyst at work; it is a vivid ceremony of courtship, barely disguised.

This passage, and others like it, characterize the late stages of the relationship between Rank and Nin. They support Stephanie Demetrakopoulos' contention that Rank "would recreate her in his own image" and "live parasitically on her life force."[6] The relationship turns into one in which Nin becomes Rank's confidante. To her he confesses his needs and frustrations:

I have always been a prisoner of people's need to confess. I do not want to receive confessions any more. I am tired of giving myself, of being used by others. I want to begin to live myself. I am rebelling against sitting all day in an armchair listening to people's confessions. I want to be free, Anais. I am never permitted to be a human being, except with you. (II, 10)

Rank was admitting to the same sort of feeling of self-annihilation that Nin had complained of. To some extent, he had helped free her from the demons of subservience and guilt — had helped her accept the Sabina side of herself. Now he strove for the same kind of freedom, and he turned to her. Nin, in response to this need, took on some of Rank's patients and tried to help him balance his life between the claims of his work and his growing desire for freedom. Nin had come to exemplify the self-cured neurotic of Rank's theory. He admired her trust in her feelings that he had himself helped to engender, but couldn't duplicate: "You are great in life as I am in creation. You lived my creations. And in that sense you are greater, and your philosophy of living is true" (II, 26).

Yes, there are hints that Rank is very much in love, but Nin — the editor of her diary — is never explicit here. We have to look elsewhere to complete the picture. Where the published diary is reticent, Nin's early fiction is more richly suggestive.

Many passages in Nin's novella, "The Voice," are in striking parallel to passages at the beginning of the second diary volume, including the long passage already presented. The story centers around Djuna, Lilith, and the Voice — a psychologist to whom these women turn for help. As Bettina L. Knapp points out in her book *Anais Nin,* "Lilith is an aspect of Djuna."[7] Anyone familiar with Nin's work will see that Lilith is an extension of Sabina (first named Alraune) from *House of Incest* and that Djuna is an extension of the *House of Incest* narrator. (That is, Lilith is that part of Nin that identifies with the dominant traits of June Miller as recorded in volume one of the diary.)

In the story, Lilith feels that she is falling in love with The Voice, but Djuna warns her that this is a mirage. No one, however, warns the Voice — or counsels him about the nature of his love for Lilith. "Do you think Lilith loves me?" he asks Djuna. "If Lilith loved me

I would give up all this and begin a new life. I want to give up analysis. Otherwise I would go mad" (p. 152).[8] This love cannot come to fruition for many reasons, including what Nin describes as the great chasm between the professional personality and the human being who is cloaked in it:

> But when he was not being the doctor, she discovered, he was not a man but a child. He wept like a child, he raged, he was filled with fears, he was possessive, he complained and lamented about his own life. . . . The human being hidden in the healer was stunted, youthful, hysterical. As soon as he ceased to be a teacher and a guide, he lost all his strength and deftness.

*   *   *

> He wrote inchoate love notes with ink blots, he leaped to meet her in the street, perspiring and nervous. He was jealous of the man who washed her hair. The child that she awakened in him was like the child in those who had come to him for care, unsatisfied, lamenting, tearful, sickly. (p. 169)

Is this "Voice" a fictional character — or an accurate portrait of Rank's behavior toward Nin? Given Nin's working habits at this time, it is probably both.

Elsewhere in the story, The Voice counsels Lilith about her name:

> Do you know the meaning of your name? It's the unmated woman who cannot be truly married to any man, the one whom man can never possess altogether. Lilith, you remember, was born before Eve and was made of red clay, not of human substance. She could seduce and ensorcell but she could not melt into man and become one with him. (p. 162)

It was to make something he could control of Nin's Lilith side that obsessed Rank. He needed to mold that red clay to his own needs. In
fact, in the summer of 1934, Rank behaved in a way that predicted
his later, more obviously possessive behavior.

At that time, Rank introduced Nin to another one of his patients,
Chana Orloff, a sculptress whose work he admired. Orloff's studio
was filled with statues of pregnant women, and Nin was pregnant at
this time. Nin writes, "Chana Orloff wanted to sculpture my head
and Rank promised her I would come" (I, 332). After a series of
sittings, and after the still-birth so evocatively recorded in diary and
story, the sculpture was finally completed. Rank, about to leave
for the United States and having extracted promises from Nin to
help him start a new life there, calls: "He is exultant because the
sculptured head of me . . . will be exhibited. He has purchased it
for his library" (I, 352).

In this incident, in the framing of the story about The Voice, and
in between the lines of the diary, we can see the pattern of narcissistic love: a Pygmalion situation. The reflection, the living reflection
of Rank's philosophies stood before him in the person of Anais Nin,
a woman whose movement toward psychic balance he had aided
considerably. But he could not let go of what he had made. He needed
something back that Nin was not prepared to give. He tested his power
with growing demands, and the relationship faltered.

Rank was playing out the old myth of the man creating the woman.
While he was intellectually aware of the debilitating consequences
of this pattern, he could not manage to resist its dynamic. In writing about *House of Incest,* Rank had ventured that the fable illustrated
the woman's "attempt to find her true woman self in this immense
man-governed factory which turns natural woman into the most demanded female types." ". . . The fundamental lie," Rank wrote,
"the real falsification is . . . the man's who first of all usurps all creation and then creates woman — whose creature *he* is — out of his rib
or his brain in order to blame and punish her for what she has become through him" (*JORA,* 73-74).

To some extent, there was an Anais Nin created out of Rank's
brain. This idealized Nin lingered with Rank in spite of his admira-

tion for Nin's self-creative action and responsibility — her Alraune nature. And Rank seems to have wanted her in all the proto-typical ways: as a mother, a mate, as the force that would make him a man and a father.

In "The Voice," the doctor writes Lilith a long letter and slips it under her door tied to a "diminutive frog":

> "This," he wrote, "is my transformation, to permit my entrance through the closed door."
>
> But this diminutive frog she held in the palm of her hand resembled him so much that it made her weep. Indeed the frog had come just as in the fairy tales; and just as in the fairy tales, she must keep her faith and her inner vision of him, must keep on believing in what lay hidden in this frog's body. She must pretend not to notice that the Voice was born disguised, to test her love. If she kept her inner vision the disguise might be destroyed, the metamorphosis might occur (p. 166).

But neither could transform the other any further. What Rank had freed in Nin could not be captured, and what lay trapped within the doctor could not be released. If Nin had had a vision of a prince, she would have to abandon it.

After spending a half year in New York working with Rank, Nin returned to Paris, their relationship seriously strained. At the request of her patients, she came back to New York during the winter and spring of 1936, encountering Otto Rank for the last time. He was working as strenuously as ever, leaving little time for himself. But he was reconciled to his habit: "I am too much of an absolutist for life," he said. To many of his questions Anais Nin replied: "I don't know, I don't live by analysis any more, but by a flow, a trust in my feelings."

"I envy you," said Rank.

NOTES

1.   Jessie Taft's *Otto Rank* (New York: The Julian Press, 1958), the only biography of Rank yet available, is the source for this paragraph.

2.   All references to and quotations from *The Diary of Anais Nin* are from the following volumes and will hereafter be indicated by volume and page number:

Vol. I *The Diary of Anais Nin: 1931-1934*. Edited and with an Introduction by Gunther Stuhlmann (New York: Swallow/Harcourt, Brace & World, 1966).

Vol. II *The Diary of Anais Nin: 1934-1939*. Edited and with an Introduction by Gunther Stuhlmann (New York: Swallow/Harcourt, Brace & World, 1967).

3.   Paris: The Obelisk Press.

4.   This preface was printed in *The Journal of the Otto Rank Association*, 7 (December, 1972), 68-74. It is accompanied by a preface to Nin's childhood diaries, also by Rank. Later reference to *JORA*.

5.   Collected in Rank's posthumous *Beyond Psychology* (Philadelphia: E. Hauser, 1941; rpt. New York: Dover Books, 1958). See also Sharon Spencer's "Delivering the Woman Artist from the Silence of the Womb: Otto Rank's Influence on Anais Nin," *The Psychoanalytic Review*, 69 (Spring, 1982), 111-129.

6.   "Archetypal Constellations of Feminine Consciousness in Nin's First Diary," *Mosaic*, 11 (Winter, 1978), 133-134. This is a special issue, The World of Anais Nin, edited by Evelyn J. Hinz.

7.   (New York: Ungar, 1978), p. 91.

8.   Quotations from "The Voice" refer to the Swallow edition of *Winter of Artifice* (Denver: 1961).

Anais Nin and Feminism
by Anna Balakian

For more than two decades the women's liberation movement has identified Anais Nin as one of its role-models. The publication of the segment of her life-long diary, numbered volume III (1923-1927) of the series called Early Diaries and subtitled "Journal of a Wife," appears to be the most revealing of the crystallization of her personality and at the same time the most closely related to the universal struggle of women to combine marriage and a career. But in her self-observation of the daily confrontation of two desires at cross-purposes, she transcends the politics of liberation to venture into its metaphysics.

The order in which Anais Nin's recent readership has had access to her diaries was to start with a volume that went back to the year, 1931, to continue through six volumes to 1974, approximately to the active stage of her illness which ended in her death in 1977. The posthumously published volumes created a flashback to her earlier years showing the development of the physiognomy of the writer and the writing, the passage of the personality from essence to experience, the motivations and their gradual realizations. If the early notations in the journal provoke surprise for readers who know the direction that her life was subsequently to take, they also explain the texture of the metamorphosis she effected as she moved toward the fictionalizing of the life which the Nin novels constitute.

Although there is one more gap, in the form of one more volume, to be filled before the kaleidoscopic portrait is complete, the unfolding of the personality and the development of the craft of writing occur before the eyes of the reader of the flashback volumes covering the childhood diary, Linotte, and the three encompassing her portrait of the girl, the bride, and the wife.

The totality of this diary is no doubt the most comprehensive document of an author's life available in the literary tradition, even

more complete than Proust's search of his past, or of Amiel's journals
to which Anais Nin refers frequently in the *Diary of a Wife*. What
makes her journal unique is its "on the spot" recording of events
and thoughts. It is less self-conscious than Gide's journals and less
apologetic than Amiel's of a century before. She is neither trying
to shock her public by candor as Gide did, nor deploring the triviality
of such recordings of caprices and confidences as did Amiel when he
wrote:

> A private journal is a friend to idleness. If frees us from the
> necessity of looking all round a subject, it puts up with every
> kind of repetition, it accompanies all the caprices and me-
> anderings of the inner life, and proposes to itself no definite
> end. This journal of mine represents the material of a good
> many volumes: what prodigious waste of time, of thought,
> of strength! It will be useful to nobody and even for myself
> — it has rather helped me to shirk life than to practice it.
> A journal takes the place of a confidante, that is, of friend
> or wife; it becomes a substitute for country and public.

By contrast, this particular volume of the rising consciousness
of a young woman who desires to shape her own destiny goes beyond the illumination of her own personality to leave us a compelling
case history for the rise of feminism, juxtaposing what the concept
meant to Nin with the reader's knowledge of what feminine liberation has come to mean in the latter part of the twentieth century.

The action takes place in New York and Paris, and it encompasses
the first four years of a marriage conceived in idealism: "I know that
this marraige, with all its little sacrifices, is the most beautiful thing
that life can give one" (p. 107). It is an epithalamium, an anatomy
of marriage, a tribute to the perfect — almost perfect — husband,
and yet it conveys the awareness that even the most perfect experience in life is as ephemeral as life itself. And with this knowledge
dominating her mind, Anais records the seismographic variations,
tries to resist, to correct, to transcend and overcome the nefarious
effects of the ambivalences of what we naively call *a* personality in

the singular form of the noun. On the contrary, it is in this period of her life that she begins to recognize the pluralism of that word, and "personality" becomes personalities: contradictory, multifaceted, changing, uncertain, inconsistent: "With my journal, I may grow accustomed to recognizing the expression of the contradictory forces of my character" (p. 176). This recognition was to be the basic factor of her delineation of characters in her novels, which she later compared to the multiple figures of Duchamp's painting, *Nude Descending a Staircase*. This volume is clearly the blue-print for the reality of that future fiction.

True to the journal pattern, Nin comments on the sundry personalities that cross her path, many of them encountered in previous volumes of her growing-up period; to these are added for the first time acquaintances from the literary world: for instance, John Erskine, now almost forgotten, but in the 20s and 30s of best-seller stature. She also records her tribulations over her father's marital problems, ponders over her own relationships with her family and in-laws. But the larger issue overshadows all these unavoidable family situations. The major concern is one over which she can exercise her will but knowing full well that each voluntary decision is apt to trigger consequences over which she will have less and less control. The issue is: how to preserve personal liberty for intellectual growth and its harvest, the while sharing and giving of self in the context of a marital union coveted and cherished. Her repeated expression of dislike for the French novelist, Stendhal, can only be understood in the light of Stendhal's attitude toward the education of women: "Not one of us but would prefer a servant rather than a blue-stocking as a life companion" (*On Love*).

As Anais Nin's beloved and supportive husband becomes more and more "the banker," and as she assumes more and more of the duties of a housewife, she perceives and is tormented by the fact that both of them are losing something infinitely more precious while performing efficiently in the roles normal to their marriage — as the state of marriage was conceived in their era. His salary rises by 75% and she proves herself an excellent homemaker; what propitious assets for a strong marital alliance, one might well exclaim. The union is presumably strengthened also by the fact that in one's free time one can share the reading of books, mutually enjoyed, walk along the quais of Paris, be selective about one's social life, have quick access to loving relatives upon demand. What else is needed for a shared life to be deemed "happy?"

But a close assessment of the diary of a wife by the diarist herself reveals flaws in the happiness. The penalty for those moments of release from chores seems excessive to the timid and sensitive wife who takes note of her every conscious movement as well as of every unconscious tropism, of every revulsion justified or unjustified as she tries to live her life in her two roles of wife and writer which move farther and farther away from each other. As she does her daily chores while he attends to his banking duties, a gnawing feeling rises in Nin. It is the basic theme of this book: are life's material obligations stifling the individual creativity of the two intellectually compatible partners? And if the wife, finding herself in a better position to cut corners on her share of the practical burdens, advances in her creative work, is she doing it at the expense of the partner less able to assert his own personal inclinations? Which one is to be sacrificed to the other? When she slackens her rate of writing he is disappointed. He says to her: "I feel part of the object of my work is lost. I work so that you may create for both of us." The question of the expendability of the one for the sake of the other rises above the problem of women's rights. It becomes a moral question over which Anais Nin struggles through three hundred pages of the diary, arriving at no satisfactory solution but giving the reader a forewarning of the direction that her destiny was to take.

What at first sight may seem the portrait of a young woman seeking her self-development is actually not limited to her sex. It is part of the larger rebellion of individuals of talent of either sex against the social condition to which the middle-classes are bound. Indeed, looking at the situation historically, one might suggest that if the proletarian upheavals of the early years of this century gave the people the right to work, the middle-class intellectuals did not get their share of benefits: that is the right *not* to work in the ordinary sense of the word *work*. Anais Nin's underlying protest in this diary is of the same timber as that of the Surrealists of the same years who rejected the nine-to-five routine. It is strange that while Nin was very well-informed about the literary output of the era, reading about seventy-five books a year, as she observes, she makes not the slightest reference to the young Surrealists who were scandalizing Parisian literary audiences with their non-conformity to the mores and economics of the times. Among the abominations they denounced were the bonds of routine employment. If for the general population liberation meant economic security and labor rights, for the artist or intellectual of non-independent means the supreme right would be liberation from a standardized work schedule. It was a desire beyond society's power to grant.

André Gide, a contemporary of Anais Nin, in the Paris of the 20s, concerned about the paradoxes of personality as deeply as Nin, could afford the luxury of a lifetime of deliberation about his complexities and contradictions and harvest whatever literary works emanated from his meditations on the self. But his was a stable economic independence, as was Marcel Proust's, and that of a number of other flourishing fellow-writers highly placed on the socio-economic scale. Moreover, they did not have deeply grounded attachments to sexual partners. The giving of self was, indeed, a public act, subsidized by private resources. The nine-to-five yoke did not touch them. In the case of Anais Nin and Hugh Guiler the impossible liberation from the economic exigency that stifles individual talent was to be the harbinger of dangers in their relationship.

Another problem, closer to women's liberation questions, lurks beneath Nin's introspective annotations of her psychic seismograph. Like Gide, she discerns in her character the conflicting currents of puritanism and Latin sensuality. Though racially Hugh was more Puritan than Anais, she observes, "I feel myself more puritan than he is, more serious, painfully serious" (p. 159). She also admires "restraint and polish" (p. 143) and has a "puritan detestation of idleness" (p. 139). On the other hand, she loves physical beauty, body movements, lush colors; but there is a level of sensuality beyond which she recoils, and her resistance to such sensual excesses brings her a certain anxiety which is not characteristic of the puritan mystique: "My reaction to sensuality causes me infinite pain" (p. 143). Behind her relentless self-analysis is the need to strike a balance between two inherent but opposite tendencies: the intellectual and the sensual reactions to life; she has to solve the conflict if she is to arrive at a satisfactory sexual behavior in her marriage for she is obsessively conscious of the dangers and failings of a too pure approach to marital relations. In her preoccupations with these trials and errors, she is not self-serving. She examines with lucid eye her own variations and weaknesses in a form of autopsychoanalysis at a time in her life when admittedly she had not yet read Freud. Out of her pages Hugo, or Hugh as she calls him in this volume, emerges as the most patient, devoted, tolerant, self-effacing hero of a husband: "The man I pity most in the world is my husband. What a life I lead him! Not a moment's rest" (p. 249).

Today's readers, exposed as they are to the women's movement, to equal rights of employment, and sexual autonomy, may find Anais Nin's self-awareness egocentric and symptomatic of her burgeoning, rudimentary feminism; but a closer scrutiny of her motivations, of her accelerating alarm for the plight of her exemplary husband, places her struggle with self and the behavior of that self above both the obsessive narcissism in Gide and the self-liberation identified with the feminism of a later period. Her observations are, in fact, interrogations on the human condition over and above self-consciousness about sexual differences. Her impatience and disappointment have to do with the value system of Parisian life; they are compounded by her subsequent cultural shock of rediscovering the raw character of New York City in the 20s. In fact, it is in this stage of the diary that she becomes aware of her total detachment from all regionalism and, indeed, from nationalism as a whole. "Hugh laughs at me and asks me what I am. Not American, that is certain, not French, not Spanish. That fits my philosophy to perfection — the fact that neither in reality nor in feeling do I belong to any nation" (p. 78). That feeling was much attuned to the spirit of the times. If ever there had been a chance for world peace, it was in the period between the two World Wars when even those directly identified with a specific national heritage were trying to find a non-national psychology to achieve international brotherhood; the tendency was particularly prevalent among the multinational artists who had made of Paris their non-national mecca.

But later in her fiction, Anais Nin was to compensàte for her geographical detachment by the creation of her own space, imperatively reflecting her own physiognomy — "au pays qui te ressemble" as Baudelaire had said. That is the intrinsic meaning of the collective title of her fictions: *The Cities of the Interior*; one brilliant such interior is the Golconda of *The Seduction of the Minotaur*, a fictitious space vaguely identified with Mexico, and having a varying topography according to the configuration of each character encountered.

The restlessness, the shedding of national bonds, of geographical anchors, have nothing to do with gender gaps or genetic, racial conditionings of attitudes. The basic cause for her restlessness is the fact that whether man or woman, whether in Paris or New York, a person of her socio-economic category is trapped as an artist, her independence in the performance of her art curtailed. She cannot devote full time to an exceptional talent except at a high cost to another individual, equally talented, to one whose own freedom may thereby be jeopardized or dangerously limited. "The few of us who revolt, who aspire to be more than beasts of burden, are punished by the futility of our longing for emancipation" (p. 68). Compounding the remorse she feels for robbing a dear one of his own independence, is her feeling of unworthiness: "Why do you struggle to detach yourself from the stupid life when you have no right to enter the other?" (p. 245) And above all, for Anais Nin, educated in Emersonian philosophy there is the problem of shaking the ideal of self-reliance.

Along with this larger issue, Anais tackles the intricacies of sexual behavior, directly questioning her perception of the pitfalls of male-female relationships: the subtle differences between friendship, flirtation, sharing of affection, and the waverings of loyalties. For most of this volume of the diary hers is the portrait of the irreproachably virtuous wife: "I know that this marriage, with all its little sacrifices, is the most beautiful thing that I can give one" (p. 107). Yet the fact of the matter is that she knows other loyalties; she responds to emo-

tions emerging from the deep well of her intricate girlhood relationships, sparking other emotional needs from time to time. And she
begins to wonder to what degree any heart, male or female, can be
shared and yet given whole to the one to whom it is committed in what
is for her a sacred communion. Since her readership consists at this
point in time mostly of persons who have read the end of the story
before its beginnings, these struggles in flashback may provoke a
certain cynicism. But future readers who will tackle the diaries in
chronological order will be deeply moved by the conflicting forces
of a complicated character who is both a solitary person and a gre-
gariously generous giver of emotions, who believes human propen-
sities to be variable, yet is dedicated to monogamy. Her doubts and
tribulations can be likened to those of a devout sectarian, for the
waverings of a believer are always more agonizing and compelling than
those of the *libre-penseur.*

What emerges from the diary is two contradictory facets of married
life. On the one hand, she has extolled the total interdependence
of herself and her husband: "How alike we are. We love the same
books, the same people, the same ideas, the same pleasures, the same
plays and walks and places. Both of us are jealous, dependent on the
other, lonely with other people, serious but happy, free only with
each other" (p. 226). On the other hand, she admits: "I make continuous efforts to link our lives, but they are too different. I must
have my life apart from his during the day, but I dedicate it to him
by filling it with occupations centering around him. That is the way
I keep near him. I want to stay near him, but I can't. A million things
draw me away. I want to be a rover; I want nobody to expect happiness from me. My very real self is not wifely, not good. It is way-
ward, moody, desperately active and hungry. I control myself only
because I love" (p. 208). Her final compromising decision gives premonition of the diaries to come; it also makes of this diary the source
book for her major novel, *A Spy in the House of Love.* "I shall live
a life, outside of ours, for the sake of ours" (p. 257). The Don Ju-
anesque character she fashioned for Sabina was to be a product of
Nin's notion of the inevitable pluralism of the self.

This volume is the closest of all the diaries to the autobiographical genre. She is not yet the magnet of literary circles. She gives us a *pas de deux* rather than a total ballet. She presents an Anais Nin totally candid and introspective, unabashed by her inconsistences; we sense the presence of the husband more often than we hear his voice. Nin's transcriptions of observations of the exterior world absorb objective realities which she has already learned to chisel indelibly into an ever enriched subjectivism. Time and again she deplores the fact that she cannot become an "objective" writer. "I could give years of my life, which I love so much, to be an impersonal writer" (p. 242). She seems unaware that in these exercises of the artist's craft she has been learning to imprint on the exterior world her personal stamp. Her suggestion of the rainy season in Paris is reminiscent of Baudelaire's *Spleen de Paris*; her description of Bruges is a finger exercises of her five senses and their acuities.

A tale of two people in two cities, the diary demonstrates their search for the spiritual life in the nameless space they want to occupy, discreetly guarding their privacy from the invasion of the very people they love best to preserve that mutually shared glow that love generates. Her book on love is both more tangible and more vibrant than that of Stendhal. In her literary future Anais Nin was to write of many adventures, many encounters. She was to transfer many of the facts and events of her life to the modes and frames of fiction. But nowhere else was she to capture that tenderness, make a more poignant and forceful bid for individuality, for the exceptional existence she thought to be her legacy.

The diary has been a popular genre for many reasons: it satisfies curiosity about an unusual personality, it casts a mirror — subjective though it may be — on the society of an era. This particular volume of Anais Nin's Diary does much more. It provokes reflection on a basic problem of our culture that she grasped in the kernel and that today passes from the category of the exceptional case to universal concern. The current definitions of "women's liberation" appear limited before the larger issues Anais unwittingly opens up in the "Journal of a Wife." She invites a more comprehensive consideration of the subject.

Her self-analysis confirms this writer's long held conviction that under the slogan of "equal rights" the women's movement has pursued a very superficial notion of what these rights may be: the goals have been too sexually oriented, too much directed toward material gains, too much centered on competition between genders. The human rights that woman's assertion of her individualism has brought into assessment can neither be secured nor protected by legislation. This woman's struggle to be free and yet to share the freedom with a loved person makes the Diary a veritable *Bildungsroman* where giving and receiving are aimed to produce a delicate balance. Many young male writers have put such anxieties into fiction form; in comparison, very few women have been able to do so.[1] Anais Nin's *Bildungsroman* is not fiction. It was woven from the threads of her daily reality. What she wanted out of life may be viewed as a woman's awakening to her own capacities and needs to achieve potentials. What she probed was not exclusively a *woman's* problem but a general one arising out of the gradual improvement of the level of women's education. With eventual parity of education for men and women, the intellectual anxieties of women approach those previously identified only with male soul-searching. Man-made rules secured for men the supportive work of women at home; they had also been able to count on a wife's concentration on his development, assistance to help forge his success, of course for the sake of the two of them.

In his remarks about the education of women Stendhal had shirked the major problem which Nin opens up with her candor: what happens when the feminine potential demands its own development, in which case the marriage system no longer supports the male advantage? Who is to suffer, who is to be supportive, who is to be affirmative? And if both play star roles, is society to be reconstructed in imitation of the system of the bees to allocate inferior positions to inferior breeds to handle the chores of the living?

When women stop being homing pigeons and become eagles if not vultures, who will be the king-makers? Who will nurture genius in the arts and sciences, who will guide the virtuoso performers and consent to self-subordination? If such self-sacrifice of one to the other is not forthcoming anymore, will the literary giants and pathblazers have to come exclusively from those in the independent income class? It is true that we have generous foundations which extend the gift of time to creative persons, but they do so only *after* the exceptional qualities have been discovered, tested, and proved. Who will tend the formative years? In our society there is more care available for the grooming of race horses than of ace-individuals, male or female. Who will take the gamble for the human potential? Who will be the man or woman to subordinate his or her own potential to the care of the partner candidly appraised as having more to give? And who will be the individual who will accept that assessment of comparative potentials without remorse? Anais's "Journal of a Wife" opens a Pandora's box of sticky questions.

What Anais Nin sensed and treasured in the person of Hugh was the heroic role of the generous husband as an integral part of woman's intellectual liberation, generous not only in economic support but in the acceptance of the fact that generosity would mean being deprived of a certain degree of companionship; it would involve the sharing of the mind and heart of the chosen woman with others. If men have taken for so long the prerogative of being in the receiving role, how many are willing to give that advantage to the woman who shares their life?

By revealing this basic issue, this volume assumes an importance far more significant for the future of our society than if it functioned simply as a diary engaging our curiosity and concern over the destiny of a single individual, even as fascinating a character as Anais Nin.

NOTES

1. A student of mine, Esther Labovits, wrote her Ph.D. dissertation on the female *Bildungsroman,* and in gathering her materials realized how few such books there are written by or on women in the process of intellectual development.

The Making of Delta of Venus
by John Ferrone

The critical reputation of Anais Nin's widely read collection of
erotica, *Delta of Venus,* has remained a little shady. Is it literary art
or, in Anais's words, "literary prostitution"? And will it in time
become respectable enough to join the company of her other fiction,
or will it, as a number of friends and feminist critics believe, continue
to tarnish her name? *Delta*'s admirers find in it some of Anais's most
alluring writing, revealing a dimension of her work that is absent from
the published diary. Yet Anais herself had no love for it and locked
it away for thirty-five years, dismissing it as a male-inspired perfor-
ance. Its astonishing success, had she lived to see it, might not have
pleased her. If the decision had been hers alone, *Delta of Venus*
would never have been published. This is how it happened.

Every reader of *The Diary of Anais Nin, Volume Three,* already
knew the story of "the collector" who in 1941 commissioned Anais
and her circle of friends to write erotica for a dollar a page, but few
people knew that Anais's manuscripts were preserved, let alone that
they were worth reviving. I first heard about them during a visit with
Anais in Los Angeles in April, 1975. By then she was being treated
for cancer, and her husband, Rupert Pole, had retired from his
teaching job to look after her and help prepare volume six of the
diary for publication. Although she was just back from a stay in the
hospital, she looked anything but an invalid, greeting me in a long red
velvet dress, her hair exquisitely arranged, as always, and held with
a spangled headband. "To cheer myself up," she said, settling into
a chair near the fire and throwing a white fur over her knees. We
talked so intently that she forgot to take her painkiller and suddenly
had to go off to bed, where she remained until dinner.

In the meantime, Rupert joined me. During our conversation he
brought up the subject of the erotica. He had unearthed the manuscripts several years before and found them enormously entertaining.

He was sure that a collection of the choicest stories would make a best seller. But Anais refused to listen. Once a year — generally on New Year's Eve — he campaigned on behalf of the erotica, and each time Anais said no.

I asked if there was any chance of my having a look at the manuscripts. "Well," Rupert said, "maybe if Anais had an editor's opinion, she might change her mind." I was only too eager to lend a hand.

That evening, after a round of martinis, I told Anais I had heard there was a best seller wasting away among her manuscripts. She cast an annoyed look at Rupert, and we laughed.

"I know that Rupert thinks it's a good idea," she said," but the writing is too imitative. No — wait for the unexpurgated diary."

It wouldn't hurt, I argued, for me to read a few excerpts, just to see if it was really as bad as she thought. She said she would think about it, and Rupert promised to gather a selection for my next visit. That was all, for the time being. We went on to talk about more important things.

It was not a matter of catching Anais in a weak moment, because nearly a year passed before I read a word of the erotica. In the months after my visit we continued work on the diary and on the essay volume called *In Favor of the Sensitive Man*. We may have talked about the erotic by telephone — we called back and forth every other week — but there is only one reference to it in our correspondence from this period. It implied, at least, that Harcourt Brace Jovanovich would be the publisher, if it were to be published at all.

Rupert gave me frequent reports on Anais's health, which would improve one week and deteriorate the next. Her voice was ghostly over the telephone, and she sometimes protested that my editorial queries were draining her limited energy. Despite this, she was helping a young California artist, John Boyce, publish a volume of erotic drawings that included quotations from her diary. The project may have brought her a step closer to releasing her own erotica, but in light of what followed, she apparently still had misgivings.

In early January, 1976, she telephoned and told me that she had decided to give the erotica to Boyce's publisher. I was stunned. Did she think it would do better with a more commercial publisher? I asked. (I should have known it had nothing to do with money; Anais had no head for business.) No, she said, it was just that she felt the erotica wasn't literary enough for Harcourt Brace Jovanovich. Did she actually mean it was too *scandalous* for us? Flattering though it should have been to hear this, I knew that few publishing houses could afford piety. I pleaded with her to do nothing until I could visit her the next month. She agreed to wait.

I arrived on February 23rd, two days after her 73rd birthday. It was a shock to see how frail she had become since the previous year. She was almost entirely confined to bed now. Chemotherapy had temporarily taken her glorious hair, and she wore a wig that looked out of character. As soon as we began to talk, she was Anais again, somehow able to levitate above the physical ravages.

"I was so sure it wasn't literary enough," she said apologetically,

That afternoon Rupert brought me a folder labeled "The Hungarian Adventurer," and while Anais napped, I read. When I finished the first two or three stories I knew that Rupert was right about the erotica and Anais wrong. This did not surprise me, but I was not prepared for the poetic quality of the writing or its feminine insights. I had been led to believe, by Anais at least, that it was purely a parody of masculine pornography. I said to her later, "It's literary enough all right, on anybody's terms." She capitulated.

At dinner we drank a toast to the birth of the erotica. It was being added to two other books in progress: "The Childhood Diary" (later published as *Linotte: The Early Diary of Anais Nin*) and volume seven of the diary. It was tempting to think that with so much going on, Anais would have to live forever. Rupert bundled up 850 pages of erotica, which I was carrying back to New York with me.

"Do anything you want with it," Anais said as I left. "I trust you."

Shortly after I returned and the erotica had won the support of my colleagues — there was scarcely a blush — Harcourt Brace Jovanovich made an offer for it. It was quickly accepted, and I could begin work on the manuscripts. How faithful to the originals must I be? I wondered. Should I be content with a light polishing, just enough to make the stories publishable, or would I dare to revise? In the end, the material itself dictated the course I followed, and I consoled myself with the thought that Anais would have approval of the final version. But at first I was uneasy about complete editorial freedom, which I had never experienced before and which is rare in the careers of most editors. A reassuring letter came from Rupert: "Anais says, delete, patch, new titles, whatever. . . ."

Freedom brought constraint, nonetheless, and I had to keep reminding myself that these were first drafts of stories; Anais had never touched them after tossing them off for the collector. She would have been far bolder in editing. In fact, she would have rewritten, as one can see by the excerpts from "The Hungarian Adventurer" and "The Basque and Bijou" that she adapted for volume three of her diary.

Although there were a few well defined short stories in the erotica — "The Hungarian Adventurer" was one; "Lilith" was another — many had to be carved out of long, episodic narratives that contained tales within tales. They needed beginnings and endings, and often titles as well.[1] "Elena" alone was 393 pages in length. Out of it came the most substantial story in the collection, along with "The Basque and Bijou" and "Pierre." Slightly more than half of the 850 pages ended up in *Delta,* and another thirty percent was used in the second volume, *Little Birds.* The rest, about a hundred pages of fragments and trimmings, was left unpublished.

The haste of Anais's storytelling — I am sure she never looked back — was evident in the more complicated sexual scenes, where she sometimes lost track of bodies. I began to count arms and legs and other parts, in case there were extras, and for one entanglement, I found it necessary to draw a diagram. It was the most unusual editing I would ever be called upon to do. Fortunately I had a woman's help throughout. What baffled my male eye alone, Margot Mabie and I often could resolve together.

A role I had not expected to play was that of censor. It was clear from the beginning that Anais, never dreaming of publication, had drawn on the outlines of her own life for inspiration, as well as on the Kama Sutra and Krafft-Ebing. It would have been easy for readers to mistake fiction for autobiography. This was so of "Artist's Model," where Anais superimposed sexual adventure on a totally innocent period of her life. The sensual awakening of the fictional model could not have happened to the prudish 19-year-old Anais of her *Early Diary*. There were many other autobiographical parallels, some probably close to fact. It becomes evident, as one reads the final volume of *The Early Diary*, that Anais borrowed heavily from her journals for material, as she did for all of her fiction.

A readily identifiable segment occurs at the opening of the manuscript called "Maryanne," a portion of which was used as a preface to *Little Birds*. It describes the events that led to the writing of the erotica and is significant because it implies that Anais offered "the collector" two volumes of her diary as erotic entertainment before she began to improvise. She hoped, as she writes in "Maryanne," that the collector would be content with "the one and only revelation made by a woman of her whole intimate life" so that she could get on with her work. But the collector did not like the imaginative parts, the metaphysical, the poetical, and she "blushed with regret at having shown the Diary to someone who didn't want it, as a woman might blush when offering herself to a man who doesn't want her." Disillusioned, she began her adventures in the world of "literary prostitution." This episode is recorded in a somewhat different way in volume three of the Diary: "I did not want to give [the collector] anything genuine, and decided to create a mixture of stories heard, inventions, pretending they were from the diary of a woman." Was Anais too embarrassed to confess that she had exposed her diary to a dirty old man? Or is the account in "Maryanne" a fabrication? I must say, in this case, the fictional version has the ring of truth.

I could not harrass Anais with questions, and so I had to censor intuitively and from my knowledge of her past. Rupert Pole, who knew her history far better than I, was immensely helpful in spotting factual passages and the names of real people. Several names went undetected. If their owners had reason to complain, they kept silent and are now immortalized.

When the collection fell into place, I started thinking of a title. I cannot recall when "Delta of Venus" first came to mind, but I do remember telephoning Anais and Rupert for their opinion. They both liked it.

"Where did you get it?" Anais asked.

"From you," I said. "I'm sure I read it somewhere in the diary." My colleagues liked it, too, and so it stayed. Out of curiosity I searched for it through all six diary volumes. I could not find it. Many years after publication of the book I would finally discover its source.

Anais lacked the strength to write a lengthy new preface, but her story of the erotica collector, told in volume three of the Diary, was ready-made. To this she added a brief postscript, and she could now bring herself to concede that there were hints of a feminine viewpoint in the stories. I am not sure she really believed it.

What she did not say was that the famous collector was a myth, which she had only recently learned. "He" was actually an underground business, one of several operating in New York during the thirties and forties, that commissioned erotica and then sold copies of the manuscripts privately. The existence of this enterprise was verified in a letter I received shortly after publication of Delta. It came from a man who had spent years of research on a group called "The Organization," amassing thousands of pages of erotica. Possibly the work of Anais and her friends found its way into their network.

In November, 1976, HBJ's innovative art director, Harris Lewine, came up with a jacket sketch by Milton Glaser, one of the country's best graphic designers. We had agreed that the book should be handled as tastefully as possible. I was disturbed about the now famous photograph of a kneeling woman with lifted skirt. Was an illustration needed? Lewine gradually talked me into liking it — everyone else did — and I sent it off to Anais for approval. Her first reaction, like mine, was negative, but for a different reason. She found the thigh and stocking exposure unaesthetic. Luckily she showed it to young friends who had stopped by, and they immediately caught its humor. So she, too, withdrew her reservations.

Anais had reported going to a party in October, her first social outing in many months, and she seemed to be rallying at last, but by the time galleys reached her in November she was in no condition to read them. Rupert tried reading aloud, but she was under sedation, and it was difficult for her to concentrate. There was never another chance for her to appraise the erotica in its edited form.

Delta of Venus was published in June, 1977, five months after her death. Since there was no precedent for it, we hardly knew what to expect from reviewers. I was already apprehensive because no advance comments had come in from the writers who received bound galleys. Erica Jong had the good grace to call and say she was busy moving. Most of the others, including Henry Miller, did not bother to reply. (Miller, I was told, later became terrible envious of *Delta*'s success, which may account for his harsh remarks about Anais, in private and in print, towards the end of her life.) The only writer who sent a comment, in fact, was Alice Walker. Aside from noting certain Millerisms in the writing, she said that *Delta* was *"the* missing piece of Nin's work." It was an accurate observation. Anais had indeed suppressed her sexual life from the published diary, the discovery of which still angers feminist readers, although she had explained her motives publicly and repeatedly.

The first indication of *Delta*'s future came from the Virginia Kirkus Review Service, seldom kind to Anais's work, which said, "The unknown client who paid Anais Nin a dollar a page back in the 1940s to write erotica got his money's worth and to spare." With publication came Robert Kirsch's fine review. "Whatever she touched took on the elegance of her way of looking at life," he wrote. "[These stories are] as readable and persuasive as some of the best of Isak Dinesen . . . delicate and sometimes, gothic, always suffused with emotion and with the evocation of setting and place . . . she found a style as rich and compelling, as filled with ambiguities and hauntings as the best of the elegant French writers of erotica." The seriousness of this review would have startled Anais, but she admired Kirsch, and he, if anyone, might have taught her to love her outcast.

There were few dissenters among the other reviewers, and *Delta of Venus* went on to become a best seller, appearing on The New York *Times* list for thirty-six weeks. It was a triumph that came too late for Anais and for the wrong reason. How would she have felt about it, Herbert Mitgang asked me, during an interview for the *Times*. It would have amused her, I said; but I was mistaken. The amusement would have been bittersweet at best. Anais could not have failed to see the irony of her success. She had battled for years for acceptance as a writer, and she was being cheered for something she had written as a joke. More royalties would pour in from the sales of Delta than from all of her previous books put together. Eventually people would read it not only in English and French, but in German, Italian, Spanish, Portuguese, Finnish, Dutch, Japanese, Icelandic and Serbo-Croat. Wasn't this simply another, more perverse example of the literary world's insentivity to her genuine life's work?

What Anais failed to consider is that after twenty-five years of diary writing, she had developed extraordinary facility for narration and psychological insight. Even when she was writing to order her natural gifts were performing. The reader of Delta is delighted to find elegance of style and feminine sensibility applied to a literary form that was often gross, dehumanizing and superficial. Despite Anais's claim that she wrote the erotica tongue in cheek, there are moments in a story like "Elena" that go too deep for plain fun. (Was she paraphrasing passages from her unexpurgated diary?) Another thing she failed to take into account was the historical context of the erotica. When she was fearlessly creating stories about Parisian brothels, lesbian love, and drug addiction, the women authors America was reading were Taylor Caldwell and Frances Parkinson Keyes. In this, as in her other fiction, she was alone, breaking new ground.

If nothing else about Delta had proved gratifying to her, Anais might not have resisted a smile as the parade of jacket art from foreign editions arrived: from Spain, a pair of comic-strip legs; from Yugoslavia, the armored torso of a woman; from Germany, mountainous breasts. Foreign publishers seemed to have lost their way in "delta's" geography. But a number of them chose to use the American jacket, and it has become a familiar sight around the world.

Five years after publication of Delta I came across notes I had jotted down after a meeting with Anais at her apartment in New York in June, 1974. Our conversation was interrupted by a telephone call, and I was puzzled by her responses. She returned laughing and said, "That was a Polish poet who works for Air India." She went on to explain that they had gone to an exhibt of erotic art by a Swiss sculptor. "Famous vaginas. Gertrude's vagina. Alice's vagina. Very witty," Anais said. Someone told a well known writer that her vagina was also on exhibit, which understandably alarmed her. Anais now had the task of calling her to say she was being teased.

"They were not really vaginas," Anais said to me, "and after a while they became rather monotonous to look at because the basic shapes were all the same — the delta of Venus. But we laughed a lot."

There it was — Anais's phrase, after all. I felt relieved. She laughed a lot, too, in the pages of the erotica, an element that, inexplicably, escapes many readers, but perhaps it is because those who know her only through her diary cannot believe she had a sense of humor. When we parted that night in June, she said, "We always have a good time together," which she always said and which was always true. It was so good a time that I went home and put it down on paper. In a sense, it was the spiritual beginning of Delta.

Since Anais's death and her absence from college campuses and feminist meetings, her following has diminished. If Delta of Venus has done the unexpected good deed of bringing about publication of her diary in countries where she was virtually unknown, it could also work against her should it, through sheer popularity, come to symbolize Nin, the woman and writer. Anais could have put it in its place. From the very start of our debate about the erotica's literary value, she seemed to be saying, "It was mere play; not my true self. You will see . . ." It is well to remember what she wrote in her postscript to the preface of Delta: "If the unexpurgated version of the Diary is ever published . . . it will show that woman (and I, in the Diary) have never separated sex from feeling, from love of the whole man."

She may yet have the last word.

NOTES

1.   Anais's titles were these: "Maryanne," "Linda," "The Hungarian Adventurer," "Mallorca," "Elena," "Artist's Model," and "Marcel."

House of Incest: Two Interpretations
by Gary Sayre

Each Man
Is an approach to the vigilance
In which the litter of truths becomes
A whole, the day on which the last star
Has been counted, the genealogy
Of gods and men destroyed, the right
To know established as the right to be.
The ancient symbols will be nothing then.
We shall have gone behind the symbols
To that which they symbolized, away
From the rumors of the speech-full domes,
To the chatter that is then the true legend,
Like glitter ascended into fire.
from *The Sail of Ulysses,"*
—Wallace Stevens

I
The Neurotic "I":
The Nightmare World of Incestuous Self-Love

House of Incest is opulent with images of decay, of degeneration, of disconnection, of dissection — a dark, wry world of unrelatedness, a nightmare world of fragmentation, the inner, psychological world of the narrator, "I": "I looked with chamelion eyes upon the changing face of the world, looked with anonymous vision upon my uncompleted self." Thus, the beginning of the first part of the prose poem is the beginning of an inner journey through a world that is internal and external; the "dream" is both a reflection of the inner and outer worlds. It is a symbolic world that the narrator will never "escape" from, as she remains "trapped" with Sabina, Jeanne, and the "modern Christ" in their nightmare world of incestuous self-love: "If only," says the "modern Christ" in the last part of the book, "we could all escape from this house of incest, where we only love ourselves in the other." This is the fictive "I" of Anais Nin, the main character of *House of Incest* who, like the other characters, is as bizarre in her personal characteristics as the world she inhabits. And exactly so, for the world she inhabits is the psychological world of herself, i.e., world and self are not separate from each other in the "dream" but are symbolic reflections of each other, inseparable. Thus, any image or description of the narrator's "world" or "house" is entirely symbolic of her psycholocal condition, which is, as such images as "chains", "dead flowers", "a room without window", "a sun nailed in the roof" suggest, a condition of extreme psycholgical disturbance, a neurosis. This interpretation is further supported by the narrator's explicit judgment of the "Modern Christ": "meet the modern Christ, who is crucified by his own nerves, for all our neurotic sins". And as the 'house" is traditionally a symbol of the body in psychoanalytic theory, the nature of this neurosis is a warped or fragmented relationship between the organic energies of the human personality, a relationship which is incestuously oriented. It is a "house of incest" as these energies, symbolized by the figures of "I", Sabina, Jeanne, the "modern Christ", and the "dancer", signify in their relationships to one another and to themselves.

Thus, the matrix of the entire prose poem is the symbol of incest. *Incest* is a word that most commonly evokes the image of a mother/ son, father/daughter, and/or brother/sister relationship or act which is primarily sexual. In Freud's psychosexual theory of personality development every child experiences early in life a sexual desire for his or her mother or father. However, incest is not really a symbol at all in the Freudian view, for a symbol in this view stands only for that which the ego cannot in reality possess; therefore, the ego creates images of the thing it wants to possess, i.e., a symbol has only as much meaning as the ego assigns to it. If *House of Incest* is entered with this expectation alone, one is going to leave wondering why the book is titled *House of Incest* since the theme of incest does not appear until halfway through the book with the introduction of Jeanne. One may wonder what in the world the pages preceding this have to do with incest, who in god's name is this figure called the "modern Christ", and what the devil is the last chapter or movement of the prose poem even doing in the book.   In an overstated way, then, *House of Incest* must express a symbolic significance deeper than the common Freudian view can penetrate, or even begin to illuminate.

And so it does.   Incest symbolizes or should I say signifies any form of self-love which is essentially selfish, or ego-oriented.   It is a love which seeks only to possess an "other" and only inasmuch as this possession be a reflection of itself: "If only we could all escape from this house of incest, where we only love ourselves in the other."   The poetic narrator of "I" articulates various forms of incestuous self-love through imagery and metaphor, beginning with the first part or chapter where the "I"'s immersion in a womb-like state of being must be viewed as an incestuous one, because it is a regression, an act produced by fear or hatred of reality, an escape from its pressures.   It connotes a state of being which is not a selflessness but a self-escape, and, therefore, a self-illusion; it is the supreme act of self-ignorance.   In general, a desire to return to the womb — the metaphor of a "golden age of childhood," or a "Paradise," or any other form of "a peace long ago" — is a desire to escape "reality" (to escape oneself), a selfish desire, a neurotic desire, an incestuous desire.

In the second part of the prose poem Sabina appears.   Sabina seeks only to possess the "I", which she does: "Around my pulse she put a flat steel bracelet and my pulse beat as she willed".   But there is something very wrong about Sabina's mysterious power: it is a power that can only consume, which, ironically, is a consuming of herself. Sabina becomes "hoarse" and can "no longer love" the narrator, for she was an unloving creature to begin with.   Her desire is carnivorous, incestuous.   She is a "harlot," period.   Her love is a lie; she doesn't love anyone but herself.   It is a self-love which can only exist by consuming others, a desire to fulfill herself by loving herself in others, a desire which is insatiable.   She is the female version of Don Juan.

Next is Jeanne, with her love for her brother.   This form of incest satisfies the conventional Freudian expectation.   The essence of Jeanne's self-love, however, contains spiritual significance beyond the superficial interpretation that her neurosis or "madness" consists

merely of her perverted desire for a sexual relationship with her brother. Jeanne is "Narcisse gazing at himself in Lanvin mirrors." She is
the female version of Narcissus but with a distinct significant symbol-
ical difference; though Jeanne and Narcissus share the essential characteristic, egocentricity, he meets the object of his self-love in the
reflection of himself; his psychological necessity is to meet his death.
Jeanne, however, can share no such fate, for she can never meet the
object of her self-love. Her brother is an idealized image of herself,
a subjectively created self-image she cannot "find" because it is without substance, without body; it is a self-illusion. Jeanne cannot, as
Narcissus did, have the madness of her egocentricity reflected back
to her; therefore, she cannot "die" and be transformed, but is damned
to move deeper and deeper into her self-created world of "ghosts
and monsters," into a self-transforming world which represents her
search for the ideal image of herself: "Worlds self-made and self-
nourished are so full of ghosts and monsters." She is herself a "ghost,"
a "monster"; her diabolical energy is a symbol of the "madness" of
Platonic subjectivism and of Jewish/Christian idealism. Jeanne is one
of "the four horsemen of the Apocalypse riding through the Bois."

The painting of Lot and his unnamed daughter is **particularly** significant in this interpretation of incest. An important figure in the
Old Testament, Lot, under the influence of wine, had incestuous relations with his two daughters, who then became the mothers of
two races of men and women: the Moabites and the Ammonites. Interestingly, in the painting the narrator observes everything around
Lot and his daughter is in flames: "great blocks of a gaping ripped
city sinking in the horror of obscenity." Even more interesting, there is
"no cry of horror from Lot and his daughter but from the city in
flames, from an unquenchable desire of father and daughter, of brother
and sister, mother and son." Why of "brother and sister, mother and
son" when the painting only depicts Lot and his daughter? It must be
that the painting symbolizes all of these incestuous relationships.
Nin seems to be suggesting that traditional Western religious consciousness is symbolized by "fire," a masculine symbol of consumma-
tion and destruction. Of course, our religions, as everything else in our
culture, are essentially rational, and, therefore, perhaps the painting

should have been dominated by light, not fire, since light is fundamentally a symbol of creation. However, Lot was under the influence of wine, symbol of an earthly, organic intoxication, and when there exists a dichotomy between body and mind, between desire and thought, between heaven and hell, then light is transformed into "fire" when the two opposing forces converge. This painting of Lot is, then, a poetic expression of the central conflict in the psychological drama, the dichotomy of dream and reality.

In the last part of the prose poem appears the most bizarre and interesting figure in this procession of symbols, the "modern Christ." His yearning to feel everything puts him in a most precarious self-loving condition; he can feel nothing because he lives in constant fear of the pain of feeling everything, though to feel everything is the desire which he clings to. He is crucified by his own nerves; he is a paralyzed, pitiable creature who can offer no salvation from the neurosis of incestuous self-love: "If only I could save you all from yourselves." Even he wants to escape from himself, but he can't. This is the supreme form of the incest motif as we experience its deepest spiritual significance in the pitiful self-loving figure of the "modern Christ": he represents the self-illusion of unbounded, unlimited desire.

Of course, all of these figures have been viewed in the light of their psychological essence, an essence which is the common thread that binds them: their incestuous self-love. But this common thread has been woven by the narrating "I", and this procession has no meaning other than that which the "I" assumes. Sabina, Jeanne, and the "modern Christ", though they have a psychological essence which distinguishes them from each other, have no significance outside of the poetic narrative. They belong entirely to the world of the "I"; they are symbols and/or archetypes of the "I"'s personality. They belong to the inner world of the personal "I," the "I" who speaks for Anais Nin. This is the "I" who speaks in the book's epigraph: "All that I know is contained in this book written without witness, an edifice without dimension, a city hanging in the sky." It is the "I" who speaks of "writing" as a "spitting out of the heart" and the "I" who continually expresses through self-reflective phrases the central conflict of the drama: the dichotomy between dream and reality.

Before I turn to an examination of this important aspect of the liberation and/or unity theme, I must further comment on the ontological abstraction of the incest motif. For true to any psychological disturbance, at the heart of each character's neurotic, incestuous state of being is a grave self-contradiction. In each of these aberrational forms of self-love, of incest, each peculiar self-contradiction spells out certain self-destruction.

The self-contradiction of the fictive "I", the main character, is her desire for peace, for a womb-like state of being, an intoxicated state of being: "the drug made fine incisions." But since the narrator possesses a rational, controlled intelligence with all the premeditations and intentions this implies, such a desire creates only a world of solitude, of alienation from herself: "Distance. I never walked over the carpet into the ceremonies. Into the fullness of the crowd life, into the authentic music and the odor of men." It is a desire which creates the ultimate form of self-destruction, madness: "only the fear of madness will drive us out of the precincts of our solitude. The fear of madness will burn down the walls of our secret house and send us out into the world seeking warm contact." But still she clings to her drug, the illusion of perpetual security.

The self-destructiveness of the second form of self-love, represented by Sabina, is infertility. Infertility implies a world of death and decay, of potentialities that "rot." Of course, Sabina is not conscious of her self-destructiveness as she is not aware of her self-contradiction; desiring everything, she can love nothing. It is the narrator who, identifying with Sabina, is able to articulate through intuition Sabina's incestuous, self-destructive contradiction. Sabina, though she moves poetically through the centuries on fire with desire, consuming love, doesn't really move anywhere but deeper into her self-made abysmal state of infertile darkness.

The self-destruction of the third form of self-love, represented by Jeanne, is, of course, Narcissism. The incarnation of extreme self-love, Jeanne is so utterly egocentric that she desires nothing less than "crusades and martyrdom." However, this desire is a tragic self-illusion, tragic because her self-love is a tragedy, a love that chains her to herself because it creates a world of isolation through the unconsious or unrealized fear of being human: "I am so utterly lonely but I also have a fear that my isolation be broken through, and I no longer be the head and ruler of the kingdom." Even her fear is a choking, chaining delusion; her "kingdom," is her self-illusory world of Narcissism. This is her tragic self-contradiction: she has "such a fear of finding another like [herself], and such a desire to find one." She desires a warm human relationship but any object of her desire will reflect the image of herself, as does her incestuous love for her brother. She is impatient, full of self-illusions, bored, tired, alienated, and chained. "I do not exist. I am not a body," says Jeanne. Her self-love is the result of her fear of loving another.

And now comes the "modern Christ." His self-contradiction is metaphorically given in the dream he utters to the other characters: his world or state of being is one of a "skinless" existence, an existence open to all human sensation. It is a state of utter pain. He desires to feel everyone' pain in order to save everyone from the pain of feeling; consequently, he can save no one since to fulfill this desire would mean taking away the essence of humanity, feeling. The self-destruction of this desire is exactly what it represents: the desire to be Christ-like in the modern world, which is the Romantic ideal of the man who symbolizes or embodies unlimited desire. But observing the paralyzed, pitiable creature that he is, one sees that such a desire is a delusion, a neurotic desire, for to want to suffer humankind's pain is but to fear one's own pain, one's own humanity — to fear the very touch of a human being. Here, certainly, in the symbolic figure of the "modern Christ" is the most tragic irony of modern man's consciousness, a consciousness that has turned in upon itself only to unleash upon the world an individualism that is not freedom but imprisonment, not progression but fixation, not creativity but artificiality, not individuality but conformity. The "superstructure" of "reality," modern man's rational consciousness, a consciousness still caught in the dichotomy of body and mind, has only elaborated the fairytale of its own history. It is a world not of authentic self-love, of creative individuals expressing their individuality, but a world of neurotic

self-love, of self-destructive individuals expressing their rigid individualism. It is a world filled with incest.

Of course, this grand interpretation of the incest motif is based
on the recognition that, fundamentally, the content of the entire
prose poem reflects the dialectical marriage of dream and reality
in the personality of Anais Nin. Besides the obvious fact that the
book could not have even been written had not Nin achieved this
marriage, more specifically it is the "I's" journey from water to daylight that makes this interpretation persuasive. It is the journey of
the personal "I" who speaks for Anais Nin, of the "I" who, through
a series of psychological revelations, is transformed into the woman
whose voice is heard to articulate the aesthetics of *The Novel of the
Future.*

II

Dream and Reality: The Birth of Poetic Vision

The dialectical marraige of dream and reality, of desire and intellect, represents in psychoanalytic terms an established dialectic between conscious and unconscious, between ego and self, between the
collective forces of the instincts and the learned, personal adaptations
of the Ego. It is the beginning of the process Jung termed "individuation," a process that can best be summed up this way: the more we
become I the more we become We (the more an individual realizes
himself or herself, the more he realizes the uniqueness of others).
It is a process of becoming, of ever becoming, more an individual
and, therefore, more a human being. Such a marriage, then, marks
the birth of individuality as, paradoxically, it marks the realization
of one's own limitations. Through Sabina, Jeanne, the "modern
Christ", and the "Dancer", the "I" is transformed from her incestuous
state of being into a self-loving state of becoming. She becomes capable
of a love which desires neither to possess an "other" nor to love herself
in an "other", capable of a love which is neither selfless (egoless)
nor selfish (fixated), but a love which is spontaneous and free in the
realization of those ubiquitous, intangible winds endowed by the

psyche unto itself, the limitations of individuality.

Aesthetically, this birth of individuality marks the marriage between imagination and intellect, or imagination and reality. It is the birth of Nin's poetic vision; the "I's" journey from water to daylight is a journey from poetic formlessness to poetic vision, the transformation of the dream into reality, which itself marks a state of individuation. The central conflict of this journey's drama is the dichotomous opposition of dream and reality, a dichotomy whose marriage is symbolically expressed by Nin through the "I's" series of psychological revelations during the course of the journey.

At the beginning of this journey, Nin creates a metaphorical experience of a womb-like existence, showing that a total immersion in the dream signifies a regression into a primitive state of awareness, an egoless state in which all sense of individuality is lost. More importantly, this immersion in the dream signifies a formlessness of vision, as illustrated physically through such images as "boneless toes." "I cut the air with wide-slicing fins, and swim through wall-less rooms." The narrator's identification with the lost race of Atlantis signifies the anonymity of her vision: "My first vision of earth was water veiled. I am of the race of men and women . . ." That she "sees things beyond the reach of human eyes" suggests that she sees, in reality, nothing. Whatever is beyond "human eyes" must remain forever invisible if it cannot be given form (the dream cannot be transformed into reality when the ego is overwhelmed and lost in the psychic energy of the dream). But the narrator loves "the blanket of water flowing over all things," the "endless bottoms of peace." "There were no currents of thoughts, only the caress of flow and desire mingling, touching, traveling, withdrawing, wandering — the endless bottoms of peace." But this is a neurotic desire, a grand self-illusion. There is no control, no focus of vision, no connection with reality in such a state of the "dream." And this dream state symbolized by water (traditionally a feminine symbol of security, protection, movement, creation) ironically represents exactly the opposite qualities. It is a "veil," a "curtain," a "blindness," a "blanket" that stifles the voice", a "soundlessness", and a "loving without knowingness." Thus, as these images signify, this psychic condition that is "found again only at night by the route of the dream" (by an altered, intoxicated state of consciousness) is a state of madness, a state characterized by the dichotomy of dream and reality, a state which, through psychological necessity, moves or awakens the "I" to another level of the dream: "I awake at dawn, thrown up on a rock, the skeleton of a ship choked in its own sails."

From the metaphorical womb of formlessness (egolessness) is born a skeleton of form, of vision, but the vision, the "I", is still "choked" by the "sails" of her delusional desire. This is why, just before Sabina appears, Nin describes the split or dichotomy between dream and reality as the lining of a coat ripped open like the two shells of an oyster. The day and night unglued, and I falling in between not knowing on which layer I was resting, whether it was the cold grey upper leaf of dawn, or the dark layer of night." Now, with this realization of her divided self, of the dichotomy of dream and reality, Nin's narrator is to experience her first psychological revelation; the "I", is to encounter Desire incarnate: Sabina.

The dichotomy of body and mind cannot possibly be expressed more poetically or more dramatically than it is by Nin in the "I's" encounter with Sabina. A symbol of womanhood, an aspect of every woman's personality, in Jungian terms Sabina is the Shadow archetype of Nin's psyche, the woman all instinct, impulse, desire, impetuous and out of control: "The web of her dress moving always a moment before she moved." The narrator makes the mistake of identifying with her: "When I saw you, Sabina, I chose my body", and she is thus immersed in Sabina's energy. The energy of the body, erotic, lustful, completely swallows the rational intelligence of the "I." This is not a marraige of body and mind but merely another form of intoxication, as evidenced by the "I's" admission: "her breath on my vision like human breath blinding a mirror." But immersed in Sabina's energy, seeing in Sabina the freedom from her own neurosis, a false identification as it is an incestuous one, the "I" becomes more sharply divided: "Only our faces must shine twofold. . ." More importantly, by being one with Sabina, the "I" realizes her relationship with Sabina is an incestuous one. Her union with Sabina has created only a world of "lies" and "fairytales." She has lost, not gained, her identity: "DOES

ANYONE KNOW WHO I AM?" Insanity comes of this realization: disillusion, dislocation, oppression, dispossession — "love divided." Dream and reality divided. Vision divided. "Reality was drowned and fantasy choked each hour of the day." "Collision with reality blurs my vision and submerges me into the dream. I feel the distance like a wound." She feels the "distance" — she becomes increasingly aware of her alienation from herself and from others, of a "FISSURE IN REALITY". She is still prisoner of herself. She is in need of a mirror of herself, someone in whose reflection she can become conscious of her incestuous state of being. That someone is, of course, Jeanne.

The appearance of Jeanne marks a significant change in the poetic narrative: instead of intense, passionate, terror-sweeping passages, Jeanne's appearance is followed by cool, delicate, and even satirical passages of lyricism, as though the narrator has become a bold observer of herself. And this is exactly so, for the narrator feels related to Jeanne through self-pity and self-hatred. Jeanne is the "I's" twin sister of the night. Jeanne, too, possesses rational intelligence, but, as the "I" observes, this intelligence only fills her world with ghosts and illusions, having turned her earthly energy into a demonic form of self-imprisonment: "Her eyes higher than the human level, her leg limping behind the tall body, inert, like the chained ball of a prisoner." Through Jeanne the narrator realizes that this world, her world, her body and mind are a "house of incest," that her madness is self-created and self-nourished. In such a state of incestuous being, there can be no hope for growth, for development or for liberation from the dichotomy between dream and reality. The tree of life is "wailing its loss of its leaves and the failure of transmutation." How can she escape? Certainly not by fearing madness; this fear is itself "choking" because it is based on the same incestuous state of being. No, the escape must come through the narrator's deeper realization of her Self. This comes through the figure of the "modern Christ" and the figure of the dancer.

Wanting to know everything about himself, the "modern Christ" cannot even begin to know anything: "I want to capture all my thoughts at once, but they run in all directions." He sits "before a

note book of blank pages," wanting "to tell the whole truth, but I
cannot tell the whole truth," he admits, "because I would have to
write four pages at once, like four long columns simultaneously, four
pages to the present one, and so I do not write at all." He is trapped
in his desire for the absolute, and so lacks focus, selectivity, vision,
and identity. A symbol of feminine sensitivity beyond proportion,
the "modern Christ" serves to reveal to the narrator the neurotic
incestuous desire for absolute knowledge, a desire that she shares
with him. "The language of nerves which we both use," she declares,
"makes us brothers in writing." For the "modern Christ" to write,
he would have to "write backwards, retrace his steps constantly to
catch the echoes and the overtones." And this is exactly what the
narrator realizes she herself has been doing since the beginning of the
book, "always searching for lost sounds and searching for lost colors,
standing forever on the threshold like one troubled with memories."
The process is the same as the discovery she made through her encounter with Sabina. "But behind our lies," the narrator concedes,
"I am dropping Ariadne's golden thread — for the greatest of all joys
is to be able to retrace one's lies." She notes: "More pages added
to the book but pages like a prisoner's walking back and forth over
the space allotted to him." She has reached the spiritual dimension
of the dream, but still has not overcome her incestuous state of being.
The only thing that saves the narrator from herself being a "modern
Christ" is her awareness of her own "lies," that is to say, her awareness of her self-division, of the dichotomy between her rational intelligence, which creates these "lies," and the world of dream which
creates "ghosts." Yet this awareness cannot unify her world of self
fragments: "I am wrapped in lies which do not penetrate my soul,
as if the lies I tell were like costumes." However, at this point the
unifying force, the liberating vision, is now to come.

It is the dancer. She "sings" the common element that binds each
aspect of the narrator's incestuous self-love, each aspect of the "I's"
personality, proclaiming, "I was punished for clinging. I clung. I
clutched all those I loved; I clutched at the lovely moments of life;
my hands closed upon every full hour." Common to all of her states
of being is their static, rigid, immobile character. In each state she

viewed the organic reality of change with dread and horror, and in order to escape the reality of change, clung to ideals which, being self-contradictions, became prisons. For the "I" these ideals are the "lies" which create "solitude." To escape organic change she created artificial order. She created superstructures and in her rebellion against the tyranny of rationalism she realizes that a total state of dream is also madness, for it implies the loss of individuality. To overcome these forms of incest she must accept the life principle of change: "She relinquished and forgave, opening her arms and hands, permitting all things to flow away and beyond her." The alchemization of dream and reality, of desire and intellect, is symbolically expressed as the dancer "danced with the music and with the rhythm of earth's circles; she turned with the earth turning, like a disk, turning all faces to light and to darkness evenly, dancing towards daylight." The movement of earth, of life, is cyclical, not linear as the rational mind has proclaimed, and in relinquishing herself to this movement she enters upon the process of becoming, for all opposites are now in a dialectical relationship with each other.

This dancing movement is the daylight that surrounds *House of Incest* like an aura, for though the content and narrative of the prose poem appear fragmented, in its totality *House of Incest* is a supreme organic unity; it is Nin's celebration of the birth of her poetic vision, a vision which expresses the relativity of human character, an organic view of life and thought, a cyclical view, a love of being which is a process of becoming, of ever becoming. Such a vision must look upon the world of rigid intellectuality as an incestuous world, incestuous because it denies the very essence of our humanity, feeling, and rigid because it is an artificial world, designed to control by holding on, denying the paradox that to truly control is to let go. It is a world of individualists, not of individuating individuals. It is a vision in which the absolute freedom of the individual necessitates not a state of anarchy but rather a state of supreme order. The process of individuation is neither selflessness nor selfishness but expresses a self-love that knows the limitations of itself. The "I" is primary in existence, yes, but to enter the process of individuation is to enter the creative process of becoming more an individual. This is why *House*

Of Incest does not "end" with a traditional stamp of finality but rather suggests something more to come. . . .

Correspondence with Anais
by Judith Hipskind

From beginning to end, my acquaintance with Anais was filled with surprises. We began a correspondence in the 70s when reading her Diaries inspired me to write to her. Her work and life had a strange effect on me — for me, the process of identification with her which many people felt upon reading her work, expressed itself in a series of clairvoyant dreams. Given the role of dreams in her work, the lure of this experience was irresistible. Eventually I wrote her of these dreams, and she responded. She knew of my interests in writing, metaphysics, and palmistry, but not until 1975 did I mention astrology to her, and ask for her birth time.

In response, I had a dream in which she sent me a letter. The last page came out of the envelope torn into two wavy crescent halves. Fitting these halves together produced a chart done in blue proofreader's pencil. This last detail convinced me of the authenticity of the dream. Recalling the chart when I awoke, I noted in my journal the birth time connected with the dream chart. A few days later, I received a letter from Anais with just that birth time — 8:30 pm — listed as hers.

Anais was interested in what "the stars" had to say about her life that year and wrote me of an apparent contradiction in her chart. My response was to write her an interpretation of her chart, explaining the contradiction and adding my own insights into her chart. I was fueled by a desire to be of help in what was for her a difficult time with her health.

At this point, the dynamics of her favorite dictum "proceed from the dream outward" come into play. The results of our correspondence and the dreams were momentous. Anais sent me to her cousin Eduardo Sanchez, an astrologer who had completed many years of research but left the data hidden away in a university library. Anais's wish was that I would work with the charts her cousin had set up and not interpreted. I promised to do this.

The amazing coincidence is that the same month I wrote Anais for her birth time she received a visit in Los Angeles from her astrologer cousin Eduardo. The visit was quite an event — they were reunited after years apart and in the process she was inspired to put him in touch with what she hoped would be the link to the continuation of his own work — another astrologer, namely, myself.

The way she managed our introduction was a matter of consummate skill on her part and is a story that must wait for another time.

Astrological Influences:
Anais, Her Father, and Henry Miller

Recall Anais's whimsical words in *House of Incest*: "Tell me what the stars are saying about me. Does Saturn have eyes made of onions which weep all the time? Has Mercury chicken feathers on his heels, and does Mars wear a gas mask?" Anais had a deep appreciation for the meaning of "the stars", a term she often used to refer to astrology's principles and interpretation. Each planet represents a symbolic function and a distinct condition, as **Anais's words imply.**

Symbolically, Mars stands for an initiating principle, energy which is traditionally depicted as masculine. Jupiter's energy entails an expansion principle, while Saturn's energy is that of the builder, formgiver whose ends necessitate the principle of contraction. Uranus, Neptune, and Pluto, the "outer" planets," represent energies which are transpersonal or collective. Their symbolic functions are distinct. Uranus denotes surprise, the original, the inventive or eccentric; it is a harbinger of the new. Neptune is aligned with the principle of illusion, with dreams and inspiration. It breaks everyday boundaries and restrictions. Pluto's energy takes the action of Neptune further, symbolizing the destruction of the old, a clearing away which allows new seeds to be planted. Our personal actions and desires take place in the arenas tended by the outermost planets. Venus represents the affectional nature, aesthetics, the feminine principle, while Mercury encompasses the reasoning powers. As in mythology, Mercury functions as a messenger; its placement shows one's way of thinking and the manner in which information is received.

In astrology the Sun and Moon are not regarded as planets, but their roles are of enormous importance. The Sun stands for the self, the core identity, while the Moon is associated with the subconscious, with deep emotions and instinct. As part of his study of synchronicity, Carl Jung investigated the role of astrological correspondence between partners' Suns and Moons and found these two luminaries did indicate a factor of compatibility between two people, particularly in the case of man/woman relationships.

Comparison of the planets of two or more individuals for partnership purposes is a very popular area in astrology, an area perhaps best seen as an interpretation of larger energies for the purpose of greater understanding of an individual or a relationshiop. There are two areas of astrological focus: indications for a relationship itself and a more subtle and extensive view that interprets the effect one or more persons are likely to have on the individual. This type of analysis is a lengthy and technical endeavor, but a brief overview of the interplay of personal energies can be obtained fairly quickly. And in the spirit of Anais's interest in astrology, here is a brief look at the influences on her growth and development found in the charts of her father, Joaquin Nin and Henry Miller. This view is necessarily selective, but the correspondences that stand out are highly interesting.

A horoscope chart forms a circle or mandala of personal expression with four compass points:

Each of the four points is a sensitive angle representing a thrust of personal energies. The left horizontal line (1) is the key to one's projection in the world and to the processes which perfect an individual's sense of self and persona. The right horizontal line (2) represents the completion of self moving ahead in time and sequence to interact with others. The innermost thinking and roots of consciousness are represented by the bottom of the vertical line (3) the results of one's perfection of self and relationships are seen in achievements, denoted by the top of the vertical line (4).

Understanding the significance of these points, one can readily see the impact of Joaquin Nin on his daughter. He was the first person to make a profound impression on her, and the astrological correspondence is compelling. His Sun (his identity) and his Mercury (the way he expressed himself) fell into direct alignment with her left horizontal line, the key to the way she chose to present herself to the world. Small wonder that at one point in her arrival in the United States she clutched a violin case so others would recognize her attachment to the artistic world. Later, her desire to communicate with her father was, naturally, intense; her self-projection aligned itself with his Mercury, or way of thinking. Communication with him would have been very much sought after as part of the process of realizing her identity.

Joaquin Nin's Jupiter, or expansion principle, was aligned with his daughter's Sun, or identity, so that his professional influence on her was a beneficial one. And his Jupiter was in favorable aspect to her Neptune, the planet of her ideals and illusions. There is a spiritual quality to this interaction between his Jupiter and her Neptune. Her mystical experience as a child of seeming to sense her father's presence as well as that of God in the communion wafer she took during church services is an expression of this particular astrological link. Clearly, Anais's father affected her deeply in her inspirations and aspirations, and the astrological indicators discussed here are all beneficent.

Further shaping of Anais's growth and expression at an adult level occurred as a result of her relationship with Henry Miller. His influence is quite apparent in the charts. Henry's Sun and Mercury also play a major, and similar, role in her chart. In this case, these two planets contact the nadir of Anais's chart, the bottom line of the four cardinal points. This means that Henry's identity and personal character traits as well as his method of thinking directly influenced Anais's subconscious. The impact of his words and expression of himself would have been enormous. But the most interesting contact is the way his Sun is related to her Moon at the nadir or root of the consciousness point. The high compatibility Jung discovered for a Sun/Moon exchange between two people's charts occurred at a key point in Anais's own chart and Henry's. Their Mercury/Moon aspect indicates his way with words; what he desired to convey universally flowed directly into her feelings and instincts. All sorts of creativity would be expected to result from this contact. .

The bottom of a chart indicates an individual's home base. In Henry's chart the Sun/Moon aspect in relation to Anais's would have invited her to perceive him as one of the family. Her urge to do things for him and to share artistic endeavors with him would seem a natural extension of the family existence she had known all her life. Henry, in his own right, had a great deal to contribute to her, as his Jupiter also contacted her Sun, her identity, just as her father's had done.

Besides representing the principle of expansion in a chart, Jupiter stands for a twelve-year cycle of experience, the same number of years as there are departments or houses in a chart, the same number of signs as in the zodiac. Thus, Jupiter connotes a special form of completion, a whole round of expanded experience that is brought home for renewal every twelve years. It is perhaps no surprise that Anais, her father and Henry Miller all have Jupiter in the same sign, with each individual poised at the beginning of a cycle that would be shared with the other. It is also perhaps no surprise that this "Jupiter effect" took place in the sign of Pisces, Anais's sun sign; this suggests that it was her identity which would bring the influences of this treble cycle to completion. This she did as a woman, and Pisces is a feminine sign.

"To Reach Out Further Mystically. . ." Anais Nin
by Bettina Knapp

"To reach out further mystically" was implicit in Anais Nin's every writing act. Such an approach enabled her to gain insight into the "occult mesmerism" inhabiting the creative experience;[1] to *know* the grandeur and awesomeness of the *numinosum*. Writing was a *rite d'entrée*, an initiation into another area of being, a deeper consciousness. In silence and solitude, like the mystrai of old, Nin experienced her way into the arcana of fresh existences: first by intuition, then through a sense of being and *participation mystique* in the cosmic whole.

"I always have to wait for an inner prompting,"[2] she declared. Whether her literary efforts were directed toward creative criticism, as they were in her *D. H. Lawrence, An Unprofessional Study* (1932), or the poetic/novella as in *Under a Glass Bell* (1941), the mystery inhabiting her inner world was revealed after contact had been made with the pleromatic sphere. Only then were the hidden truths decanted in glazed imagery; only then did symbol echo emotion; line suggest feeling; light shadow a silent happening; and rhythm thirst for the ineffable.

For the mystic that Anais Nin was, the *All* is linked, even though on the surface certain actions, sensations, and thoughts may be considered isolated; they are nevertheless dependent on a universal plan, an immense analogy. Deepening states of knowledge or awareness allowed Nin to transform the inarticulate into the object, the idea into the word, the signifyer — and in so doing, her essence was being perpetually modified by the interrelationships and parallelisms experienced. The creative act became a foray into an infra- or supra-conscious sphere resembling, to a great extent, the poetic quality described by William James:

. . . states of insight ino depths of truth unplumbed by the discursive intellect. They are illuminations, revelations, full of significance and importance, all inarticulate, though they remain; and as a rule they carry with them a curious sense of authority for aftertime.[3]

Although Nin had experienced the *numinosum* as far back as she could remember, two factors were instrumental in linking her cosmic experience to the creative process: her confrontation with the works of D. H. Lawrence and the therapeutic sesssions with Dr. René Allendy. The former allowed her to feel the "occult mesmerism" living inchoate in the artistic endeavor which she expressed subjectively in her volume on Lawrence. Her relationship with Allendy paved the way for a deeper understanding of her psyche as well as for a knowledge of alchemy, numerology, dream interpretation, and the mystical arts in general about which he was a specialist. In *Under a Glass Bell,* Nin incorporated her learning into her writing. She made the mysterious domain of spiritual/physical realities evident through sequences of insight; and similar to the illusionist of old, she transformed chaos (or the unmanifested) into cosmos (the orderly and manifested).

Nin's approach to criticism fused subjective and objective reactions. It was a visceral and spiritual experience; a *metaphysical probing.* As the title indicates, *D. H. Lawrence, An Unprofessional Study* is dual in nature. It is "unprofessional" and, therefore, violates the codes and ethics of the critic's profession. Nin rejected the systems and formulae of conventional criticism with its cerebral approach to art and life. She unleashed her moorings and cut ties with what was; but her rebellion against the status quo did not imply aimless wandering. On the contrary, her uprooting paved the way for a rerouting and rerooting into an expanded and steadier vision. Her essay on Lawrence is also a "study," and, because of this, Nin applies mental faculties to the acquisition of knowledge. Knowledge for Nin includes Socrates' statement "know thyself" as well as Nietzsche's "be thyself." She projects her unconscious world onto Lawrence's universe and via symbiotic relationships experiences the mysteries embedded. She transforms her personal vision into the collective sphere. The "universality of the subjective experience,"as Kant phrased it in his *Analytic of the Beautiful,*[4] allows a welding of personalities: Nin, as mystically oriented critic and artist, and Lawrence, the object of her scrutiny.

Nin's course was non-intellectual. Unlike such critics as Hazlitt, Lamb, or Sainte-Beauve who believed themselves repositories for collective opinions; Marmontel, who drew a cut-and-dry dividing line between beauty as it existed in nature and beauty inherent in the work of art; or l'Abbé Dubos, who suggested that beauty existed in the eye of the beholder and was a question of personal taste; Nin's way was subdued and modest. It took the form of a *sinking into self;* an *inner contemplation.*

To follow Nin, therefore, into the intricacies of Lawrence's style, the folds and lobes of his characters, the tonal harmonies and cacophonies of his inner and outer scapes, is to take a fantastic voyage; to "flow forward" with the creatures of his fantasy, to follow their feelings as manifested in impulses and gestures. Nin used a variety of techniques to chart her course: *intuition,* relying upon tropisms to understand the immense analogy which bound her to Lawrence's inner world; *synesthesia,* which opened the world of the senses; the *dream,* which allowed her to peer into subliminal spheres, to delineate in sharply focused images the colorful and subdued tonalities, the shifting shapes which emerged full blown into consciousness only to blend back like shadowy essences into the objective psyche.

Intuition, as Bergson suggested, is a direct and instantaneous way of *knowing.* The experience involves the entire being, "primal consciousness," as Nin wrote, "premental" activity which has "nothing to do with cognition" (L,2). The intuitive approach to literature encouraged Nin to sink into a text, to contemplate it as one does geological strata, to plunge into the mysterious sphere which opened to her and became the source of her creative *élan.* In these new spiritual/physical climes, the multiple fused with the one, space with spacelessness, and time with timelessness; the "unmoved mover," to use Aristotle's wording, was sensed; and non-human knowledge absorbed. Mystics from St. Augustine to Abraham Abulafia have described such intuitive experiences as a face-to-face encounter with divinity. For Nin, intuition implied a confrontation with that transpersonal force which lived inchoate within her every fiber — which gave sustenance and nurtured life.

As Bergson stated in *An Introduction to Metaphysics* (1913), intuition placed the individual "within an object," thus allowing him to coincide with what is unique and, therefore, inexpressible in the work of art. Analytical methods describe the object from the outside: they portray its features from a variety of perspectives. Then, however, Nin comments, only "the shell" or the "husk" is visible. Intuition, on the other hand, penetrates the object under study as a laser beam — it allows for heightened vision.

"Intuitional reasoning," Nin wrote, encouraged her to experience the inner architecture of Lawrence's being — the spirit as well as the body — to combine the visceral with the cognitive. Lawrence's "dark gods" are encountered as they exist subliminally in all of his characters; no longer hidden and repressed, but burgeoning, awakening to life's variegated experiences. Instincts, Nin suggests, should not be reviled. They possess their own wisdom. They transcend the thinking function and are similar to "an adroit juggler who can make everything balance and fall right." (L, 8) Sophists and casuits can argue almost any point and make it valid. Instincts do not lie. To know people is to listen to the "body"; to learn its "dreams" and its "needs."

We are at the opposite poles of Plato and the Christian ethic and aesthetic which considered the intellect to be the divine part of man and taught the subjugation of the senses, or, as Nin described it, the eradication of "the livingness of the body" (L, 9); and Nietzsche before Lawrence had considered the post-Socratic Christian ethic as the destroyer of the body (man's vital nature) and the builder of the mind which had become with time a hollow instrument: the Apollonian at the expense of the Dionysian way. Lawrence's denunciation of the Christian ethos did not imply an atheistic view. On the contrary, Lawrence was "true to his deep instinctive sense of religion," Nin wrote (L, 30). He knew God in a personal and powerful manner.

> Lawrence was in reality a profoundly religious man, in his
> search for God which he pursued all through his life, and in
> his personal conception of God. For in spite of his non-con-
> formity he realized God. (L, 38)

Lawrence and Nin experienced the sacred in life. Their God, however did not divinize the intellect; their deity was not the ethical
and sinless creature possessing moral dictates which organized religion had interpreted as a rejection of the flesh. God was an energetic force who allowed the individual a communion of body and
spirit — thus contact with life's flow and the pleromatic sphere. Both
Lawrence and Nin discarded the taboos that organized religion had
superimposed upon individuals and societies: an ossifcation of what
had once been a living and vibrant symbol and had become a "guaran-
tee' against fear. Like Emerson, they rejected external authority
and placed their confidence in an inner light. Religions for them
and for the New England transcendentalistis were "the same wine
poured into different glasses." Lawrence's and Nin's world em-
braced the universe as viewed in the Self — a composite of opposites
or the mystic's *All*.

> It remained for Lawrence, however, to give mysticism a
> rebirth in terms which have the advantage both over the
> traditional mysticism and the abstraction of mathematics
> in that he made us feel the unity in this eternal paradox
> *through our senses*. He restated mysticism in modern terms.
> (L, 96)

Not "through the eyes," Nin wrote could Lawrence's writings be
understood as seminal forces (L, 8). The eyes, lodged in the head,
spell cerebrality and scientific positivism for her, an attempt on man's
part to encapsulate the limitless into arid formulae, conceptions and
abstractions It is not "an upper plane in the head, the brain," she
continues that such an inflow and outflow of primordial sensations
and impulses can expand the poet's vision (L, 5). Rather it is in the
solar plexus. There, Nin declares, one finds "blood-consciousness,"

which causes the creative act to manifest itself. The solar plexus functions as an inner sun (solar), light which radiates in darkness and which warms remote and insalubrious realms. The sun also stands for spirit and consciousness. The plexus consists of a network of vessels, nerves, and fibers which, when activated by solar forces, sets the inner machinery into motion and commotion. When the solar plexus is touched, radiating nerve fibers take on harmony and form. In *Sons and Lovers*, Lawrence's creatures took root in preformal realms where he contacted "the source of life," multileveled states of consciousness. In *Fanstasia of the Unconscious*, Lawrence wrote: "As the night falls and the consciousness sinks deeper, suddenly the blood is heard hoarsely calling. Suddenly the deep centers of the sexual consciousness rouse to their spontaneous activity" (L, 22).

Nin, like Lawrence, searched for the "central physical vision" or "instinct" to involve and guide her to the source of creativity. A linking of "physical vision" and "instinct" includes *soma* and *psyche*: full-blooded analyses which do not kill the texture and consistency of writing, do not immobilize its shifting beats and rhythms, do not divest it of its inner flow — its sustenance which paves the way for its growth and development. On the contrary, by combining the physical and the spiritual — earth and heaven — a complete experience is lived.

The unification of polarities, such as soma and psyche, or good and evil, entails a "vitalistic" struggle which both Nin and Lawrence associated with the life force — with blood as it pulsates in powerful rhythms, reflecting and deflecting the meanderings within the individual and the collective. In *The Plumed Serpent*, Lawrence rejects the Christian Church and chooses instead the old, still-powerful, and mysterious gods. They energized his senses and his imagination, as well as those occult forces which lived within him. Man's relationship with divinity in this novel is described as an initiation ritual leading directly into the mystic's ecstatic experience during the course of which the unknown and ephemeral are transformed into the actual and the eternal — the crude sensation into the polished work of art. Lawrence's God who "is nameless and unknowable" made the fusion of man with deity possible. Deities, he suggested, manifest themselves in many forms and ways: many Gods "come into me and leave me again. And they have various wills, I must say."

For Nin and for Lawrence, God *is* that power which lives in the poet, that force which pulsates in the universe. Emerson in "The Over-Soul" described this entity as transpersonal energy:

> . . . a great public power in which he (man) can draw, by un-
> locking, at all risks, his human doors, and suffering the
> ethereal tides to roll and circulate through him; then he
> is caught up into the life of the universe, his speech is thun-
> der, his thought is law, and his works are as universally
> intelligible as the plants and animals.

Nin and Lawrence were not alone in denouncing the Westerner's emphasis on developing the intellect. In *Out of My Later Years,* Einstein (whom Nin mentions) comes to look upon the intellect as a force which blocks discovery: "And certainly we should take care not to make the intellect our god; it has, of course, powerful muscles, but no personality. It cannot lead, it can only serve; and it is not fastidious in its choice of a leader."[5] The Orientals created the *koan* which points up the limitations of the logical and reasoning principle and enables man through expanded physical and mental vision to experience a new reality; a fresh awareness by nonverbal means. Lawrence's protagonists live fully, Nin wrote. They "fall into mystic trances"; they "flare into demonic anger, brood or pass rapidly from despair to bliss" (L, 19). Their intuitive powers allow them to leap into the unknown — always authentically.

Synesthesia was also used by Nin in her critical and creative works. A sense experience used as a literary technique by Baudelaire, Rimbaud, and Mallarmé and as a powerful energetic device by such mystics as Boehme, Saint-Martin, and Swedenborg, it aids the hierophant to experience the pleromatic sphere. Synesthesia implies a unification of the senses: such a condition to all intents and purposes can exist only in the uncreated world when the five senses are one; in the manifest domain they are divided into sight, smell, touch, hearing, and feeling. To know an interchangeability of the senses, Rimbaud suggested, required a type of eruption or combustion within the inner world; then the visual may be heard, smelled, touched, or tasted or the tasted may be heard, seen, smelled, or felt.

Synesthesia may be compared to a giant awakening; a psychic happening, a flaring up of forces within the unconscious. It enables the artist to experience simultaneity of sense impressions; to see the work of art coming into being, to contact new languages, forgotten species — preformal life. Jakob Boehme and Isaac Luria had *known* such ecstatic moments when they leaped into their inner world, discovered its treasures and placed these as constellations in their writings. To allow the **synesthetic experience** to bear its full fruit, the artist must be willing to undergo a momentary eclipse of his conscious personality: a dissociation of the ego. He then permits the powers of the collective unconscious to engulf him. The inner eye and ear feel the cadences and aromas, as Nin wrote, "the bulginess of sculpture," and the "heavy material **fullness,**" expressed in rhythms as well as in "nuances of pain" (L, 78). A new creative center, an unlimited source of inspiration, is then discovered by the artist.

The technique of synesthesia allowed Nin to extract new riches from Lawrence's works. It taught her another *way* leading into his personal and objective psyche. "Lawrence's language," she wrote, "makes a physical impression because he projected his physical response into the thing he observes" (L, 71). A flow from her primitive self into Lawrence's energized a combustible state, set up the dynamism necessary to unshackle the flood gates, to activate the vortices, to illuminate the darkened realms behind gestures, feelings, and words. As a result of such swift sensorial interchange the unconscious motivations of Lawrence's characters as well as his philosophical and metaphysical insights emerged — not as abstract essences relegated to some remote ethereal clime, but as living forces in the life process. Nin writes: "His sensorial penetration is complete. That is why his most abstract thought is always deep reaching: it is really concrete, it passes through the channels of the senses" (L, 78).

The synesthetic way captures life in its flux; action in its counteraction; it transforms the idea into the act. *Change,* as posited in the Heraclitean doctrine, becomes the only reality. **The notion of perma-**

nence is an illusion, the product of sophistry, paradoxes, and casuistic reasoning. Within each entity (either organic or inorganic), both Nin and Lawrence declared, opposites exist: being and not-being. The only true state, then, is that of transition. If strife were ended, Heraclitus wrote, so would life. "There would be no musical scale unless high and low existed, nor living creatures without female and male, which are opposites."[6]

Activity, combustion, combinations and recombinations are for Nin and Lawrence the *sine qua non* of the synesthetic — and poetic — experience. To force a reshuffling of emotion requires aggressivity on the part of the creative individual; that "deep rhythmic under-current, rising to a climax when he enters and possesses the 'unknown world'" (L, 136). It pierces husks, sheers layers off conventional material and prosaic screens which hide the invisible domain. Such powerful inner activity externalizes unconscious contents, forces past experiences to imbricate themselves into present situations, alters circumstances, relationships, continuity, and contiguity. The work of art feeds on kaleidoscopic sensations. The rich nutrients it confronts pave the way for its growth and development.

The dream also allows Nin to "reach out further mystically" into the pleromatic sphere: where polarities become one; the nonmaterial acquires materiality, the vaporous grows solvent, and the present reaches into past and future. As defined by C. G. Jung:

> The dream is a little hidden door in the innermost and most secret recesses of the psyche, opening into that cosmic night which was psyche long before there was any ego-consciousness, and which will remain psyche no matter how far our ego-consciousness may extend. ... All consciousness separates; but in dreams we put on the likeness of that more universal, truer, more eternal man dwelling in the darkness of primordial night. There he is still the whole, and the whole is in him, indistinguishable from nature and bare of all egohood. Out of these all-uniting depths arises the dream, be it never so infantile, never so grotesque, never so immoral.[7]

Lawrence's characters, Nin suggested, emerged chaotic from the collective unconscious. Similarly to Cézanne's canvases to which Lawrence alluded, so he shapes and reshapes the *stuff* from which his creatures are made: not in triangles, cylinders, or cones, but within his own frame of references — blazing or dimming lights, swelling or dissolving passions. Life for Lawrence and Nin, as it had been for Cézanne, was seized in its fluidity of color, its feeling tones; articulated in tactile reverberations; silent dialogues — the soul groping to express itself.

To use the dream as a literary vehicle in the manner of Nin and Lawrence required a turning inward; a guiding of life's flow of energy into the psyche. Such a condition entails isolation. If a depth experience is to be conveyed and a new ontology delineated, fresh centers of feeling must be discovered. Isolation can help nurture such a condition. For mystics such as Boehme or Blake, writers such as Nin and Lawrence, solitude weeds out draining forces; allows the seed, the idea, the feeling to benefit fully from the nutrients needed for the growth process. The type of isolation referred to by Lawrence and Nin was not that known to the Trappist, to be sure; rather it was a withdrawal from the workaday world which allowed the artist to absorb the rich soil of his inner system, to understand impulse/sensation leading to self-knowledge.

There is a way, Nin suggested, of recording dreams. Not in the manner of some modern writers who insert into their works the dream's "triteness." In such cases, the "dream has dwindled" into sequences of "pitiful, graceless attempts" to express an inner architecture. Lawrence, on the other hand, was "patient" and listened to the murmurings of his dreams and allowed them "to find their own way and hour of resurrection;" he experienced them as fully as his nature and talents allowed. Dreams for Lawrence took a long period of gestation. He waded "through a maze of timidities, retractions, bounders, awkwardnesses" (L, 10). He succeeded in extracting the living essence from his dreams, their blood-fibers, continued Nin, because of his "confidence in the wisdom of the body."

Dreams have their own realities, pulsations, spatial concepts. They must be experienced, to use Bergson's term, as flowing and active currents rather than as congealed images or static monuments in space. They are like "vessels of steam from which live jets escape," then travel throughout the cosmos, condense, and relive their multidimensional course. Dreams are "inexhaustible reservoirs" for the creative individual who not only feels them, but cohabits with them, experiencing their moods and sensations in accordance with their level of consciousness. The dream for the ancient Egyptian, Hebrew, and Greek had mantic and healing powers. It was so important that dreams were used as part of initiation rituals. The word *initiation* ("beginning" or "entrance") affords individuals penetration into new spheres: a real inner journey of *katabasis*. Plutarch described initiation ceremonies as a descent into a "marvelous light" during which the neophyte passes into "pure realms and prairies where voices and dances resound, sacred words and divine apparitions inspire religious respect."[8]

The technique of the mystic — intuition, synesthesia, and the dream — enabled Nin to experience the "infinite nuances," the "fullness and expansiveness," of Lawrence's world. A psychopomp, he guided her into an arcane universe where she felt renewed — to a state of perpetual becoming: wherein the energetic life process became a transcendent experience.

> . . . we are born and die, we are born and die, as often as
> we have the vitality to be born again; and this movement
> is not confined to the hours between our physical birth
> and our physical death. It is an evolution of the mind
> and soul within themselves, the evolution of the universe
> reduced to the terms of our own soul. (L, 111)

René Allendy initiated Nin into the arcana of alchemy numerology, and mysticism in general, devices she later transformed into a literary technique to be found in such works as *Under a Glass Bell*.

René Allendy (1889-1942) was well known in medical circles as the founder of the French Society of Psychoanalysis, as well as the doctor who had introduced psychoanlysis into criminal court cases. He was a mystic and was fascinated with all aspects of this problem, as his thesis, *The Alchemical Theories in the History of*

Medicine (1912), indicated. Allendy was convinced that destiny follows the dictates of man's unconscious will; that his actions are often repeated because there are profound desires within him that urge him to reenact the same or similar events and situations. Man projects this inner force onto his environment and considers external reality rather than himself to be responsible for things if they do not turn out as he wishes. If man is determined enough, Allendy believed, he can control fate to a large extent. In order to do so, however, he has to understand his inner motivations. To succeed in bringing unconscious forces to the light of consciousness requires an almost Buddhistlike discipline. Allendy spoke from experience. He had been gassed in 1915 and then developed tuberculosis. The medical men at the time stated categorically that he had no chance for survival. Allendy, however, decided differently. He did not accept the destiny predicted. Not only did he succeed in arresting his tuberculosis, but he also increased his capacity for work after recuperation. He had a private practice, attended in hospitals, wrote such books as *Dream and Psychoanlysis* (1926) and *Orientation of Medical Ideas* (1932), to mention but two. Psychoanalysis, he suggested, could bring about the enlightenment necessary to permit an individual to escape from his misfortune, his *karma*.

Nin had no illusions concerning the therapy she underwent. She knew from the outset that the probing experience would be difficult; that it would entail sacrifice on her part. But life, she reasoned, is a process of transformation and requires perpetual immolation — the death of one state and the creation of another. Therapy, she realized, had to be faced with composure, courage, and consciousness.

In her *Diary,* Nin wrote that she responded to Dr. Allendy's method at first: to the "patriarchal air." He reminded her of a spiritual father, a "Shaman," an influence she needed desperately at the time to replace the void which her own father's insensitivity and egotism had created in her life.[9] Another aspect of Allendy's personality which endeared him to Nin was the interest he expressed in the plight of women in general, and hers in particular. Psychiatrists, he confessed, knew little about the functioning of women's inner world.

Women have contributed nothing to psychoanalysis. Woman's reactions are still an enigma and psychoanalysis will remain imperfect as long as we have only man's knowledge on which to base our assumptions. We assume that a woman reacts like a man, but we do not know.[10]

In addition to the therapeutic sessions, Allendy's kindness, perhaps inadvertently, was an important factor in broadening Nin's knowledge of the mystical arts. When he realized that her financial situation would make it impossible for her to continue in analysis, he thought of an alternative plan. He asked her to do research work for him. The money she would earn would be used to pay for the analytic hour. Nin agreed and spent many hours in a variety of libraries gathering information on medical and occult topics. Not only was she an invaluable aide to Allendy when he later wrote *Essay on Healing* (1934) and *Paracelsus and the Cursed Doctor* (1937), but he also afforded her the possibility of learning about the mystical arts from a serious scholar in the field. Nin took the opportunity to familiarize herself with Allendy's previous works: *Alchemy and Medicine* (1929), *The Great Therapeutic Works of Alchemists and Principles of Homeopathy* (1920), *The Emerald Table* (1921), *Symbolism of Numbers* (1921), and *The Problem of Destiny* (1927).

Allendy believed that curing the sick entailed a process of adaptation: to space, because the virus or bacteria was lodged in a particular organ or tissue; and to time, because of the malady's appearance and disappearance. He believed that psychological as well as physical ills are borne, for the most part, because of a disparity within the chemistry of one's body and the inability to adapt to one's environment. Never did he suggest, however, that therapy, no matter how successful, could rid a person of all of his ills. Like Paracelsus, he suggested that man suffers from his "mortal" condition. Once born, he becomes separated from the "Universe" and, as long as he lives, yearns to experience the primordial unity he once knew.[11] For Allendy, then, psychotherapy to a great extent was a metaphysical problem: a question of channeling one's libido (psychic energy) toward one's personal needs as well as toward cosmic ends. His notion of psychological independence, consisting of a twofold process, detachment and harmony of being, was adopted by Nin, too.

Nin also learned the metaphysics of numbers from Allendy. As C. G. Jung, so Allendy believed that numbers have a numinous quality about them. Mystics claim that numbers were not invented by the conscious mind but emerged from the unconscious, spontaneously, as archetypal images, when the need arose. Numerological associations were important for mystics since numbers were used for mantic purposes. As ordering devices, numbers are one of the most ancient representatives of man's spirit and intellect; they are also attributes of matter. Psychologically, numbers are archetypal contents; as such, they arouse energy, rhythms, patterns, and foment a dynamic process. They are "idea forces," that is, the concretization or development of virtualities or possibilities in space; they are also experiences or shapes that lie latent in the unconscious until consciousness experiences them in the form of "images, thoughts, and typical emotional modes of behavior."[12] In the conscious domain, numbers are "quantitative," in the unconscious, they are both "quantitative and qualitative," thereby triggering all kinds of sensations and feelings. As ordering devices used by man since the beginning of time, numbers are manifestations of his desire to conquer the world of contingencies, also the one that lies in his dominion. Since numbers lend order to what might be considered as chaos, they give a sense of security to those in need of it, and in this regard are considered "archetypal foundations of the psyche."[13] It is understandable that an entire book in the Old Testament should be called Numbers because within its pages are enclosed generations of souls leading back to the beginning of time, thus giving historical continuity to the Jewish people. The tracing of Christ's lineage back to David is likewise an attempt on man's part to experience his ancestral soul in its original form.

In Allendy's *Symbolism of Numbers,* he analyzes the mysterious relationships between numbers and phenomena. Numbers, he wrote, obey precise laws although these may remain unknown to man; indeed, they are "the purest expression" of these laws, which rule over all homogeneous phenomena. Crystals, plants, man, stars, suns, and chemical spectra are regulated by certain laws, all of which have their coefficients. Allendy agreed with Balzac's statement in *Louis Lambert,* that ""'Everything here on earth exists only in terms of movement and numbers; and movement is in a way a Number acting."[14] Numbers, therefore, have mysterious and elemental powers which escape man's cognition. They are understood only in their most rudimentary form: as unity (1), duality (2), trinity (3), and quaternity (4); as concepts, abstractions, and ideas. By studying the symbolism of numbers, Pascal had reasoned, that is, "the development of the idea of the Number, one discovers a key to an extremely precious analogy" which may pave the way for the unraveling of the greatest marvels in nature. For Pythagoras, numbers were a universal language, and intiates who delved into their arcana could learn "the principle of things." Allendy looked upon numbers as intermediaries between supreme thought and its materialization in the object, as the Kabbalists and Platonists had done before him.

Allendy also acquainted Nin with alchemical processes. Alchemists and metaphysicians have posited that as metals buried deep within the earth go through a physical process of change from base metals (lead) to purer and more noble forms (silver, gold), so the human personality experiences a concomitant evolution: from a state of un-consciousness,k immaturity, and irresponsibility to consciousness, maturity, and responsibility. The alchemist expresses the three phases of the transformatory process that he conducts in terms of color: *nigredo, albedo,* and *rubedo.* The psychologist translates these phases into steps in the maturation process. *Nigredo,* or the blackening pro-cess, indicates the preconscious period of psychological development, before ego-consciousness has come into existence. *Albedo,* the whiten-ing process, during which time the washing of the elements takes place, implies the birth of consciousness, when differentiation comes into existence; the I and the Thou experience each other as separate en-tities. With *Rubedo,* when the elements rise to their most powerful intensity, a union of opposites emerges: rather than the unconscious-ness of the first phase, or the conflict of the second, harmony and independence is achieved through an understanding and awareness of the polarities of life.

Nin's studies in alchemy and numerology in addition to the thera-

peutic process activated her unconscious, and she discovered her own
primitive nature, her yearnings and torments. To face *her* inner world,
however, required courage. To articulate and then record its happen-
ings in sequential visions was torture for her: it was compared to
childbirth. And the postpartum separation which followed, with its
ensuing loneliness and agitation, was harrowing. Her nights were
filled with clusters of biomorphic shapes, meandering lines, hybrid
fantasies, colored intonations, and metamorphoses of all types including crystals, metals, fire, and water. These she used in all of her
creative endeavors.

Under a Glass Bell is a composite of configurations which are im-
bricated directly in the visions described in the stories. The starting
point of Nin's hallucinatory wanderings is nearly always suggested by
some material object: glass, bell, house, or some series of sensations
such as the sun's rays or the moon's coldness. Her feelings and the
inroads these made upon her as she journeyed inward are conveyed
in spurts of youthful exultation as well as in charred and incandescent
images. Language, for Nin, now that she incorporated both the alchemist's and the numerologist's vocabulary into her own, was no
deadened instrument, but the recipient, the echo, and the receptacle
of an imponderable world.

Under a Glass Bell is a metaphorical equivalent of a state of mind.
The three protagonists, Jeanne and her two brothers, whose relationship is symbolically incestuous, become visual arrangements of a
corresponding affective condition. The *bell* sets the tone. Its vibrations echo a universal design. Its depth and mass impose a sense of
space. The bell-shaped construct takes the form of a triangle, suggesting a mystical emblem in the Pythagorean cosmogony; a trinity of
mobile lines imposed upon an unlimited expanse which is tense and
disquieting. The bell triangle representing the three protagonists in
Nin's story is the central image of a complex of appearing and disappearing sensations. It concretizes an inner necessity: a truth, as
Jakob Burckhardt wrote in *Reflections on History*:

> . . . without art we should not know that truth exists, for
> truth is only made visible, apprehensible and acceptable in the
> work of art.[15]

"The glass bell covered the entire house"[16] is a visualization of mystical experience. It represents Nin's adventure in thought, feeling, and dream — the reader's as well: that is, the reader who projects upon the image, who is caught up in its entanglements; its sheets of infra-red light hurtling, cutting, bruising, like "stalactite torches." Reader and protagonists converge, as the viewer and a painting (for example, Picasso's "Studies of Glasses") in preparation for a physical and mental involvement. The bell expresses a longing for celestial and spiritual spheres. "I am not living on earth," Jeanne says. The bell also conveys a need for earth, matter, and matriarchal over patriarchal spheres; it is a *complexio oppositorum*. The bell is motility and fixity; ascent and descent, verticality and horizontality; a linking of two conflicting forces, two polarities juxtaposed, antithetical, in crucial and cruel conflict. From the bell clusters of echoes resound; reverberations of personal and universal designs; each caught in a network of perspectives and shadows, like "icicles of the mind," as Artaud called them, clashing, blinding, burning forces. An androgynous image, the bell suggests a linking of male and female forces: it nurtures a condition of incest, endogamy, and narcissism. The visual impace of the bell sets up a correspondence between reader and protagonists: it orders chaos; confines mass within measure; firms movement; and stills sound.

Glass is hard and brittle. The sun transforms it into crystalline mosaics. It can be transparent as clear water. Nin writes in Platonic terms: it is an "external envelope which deludes others into thinking I am alive" (UGB, 37). Transparency allows for interaction between interior and exterior worlds — Jeanne and her two brothers are frozen in a single moment of time and space, yet float about; imperceptible to the reader, yet visible to him from multiple sides and by the mind's eye. Glass is a way to the soul; the point from which a central system of coordinates radiates, setting the stage for feelings of sadness, tears, and pain to prevail.

> She watched her sorrow. She looked at the Tears. The sorrow
> unveiled and reflected before her ceased to be her own. It
> was the sorrow of another, with a space between them. She
> looked at the tears and they froze and died. (UGB, 42)

Shadows, crystals, mirrors, and dark caves reverberate in alchemical
tonalities; each casting the protagonists' needs and desires outside
of the glass covering, liberating them from paralyzing forces. The
motility of this interaction suggests a drive to explore space, to eva-
porate sorrow. "The light from the icicle bushes throws a patina
over all objects," writes Nin (UGB, 36). The reader and protagonists
experience each other as clusters of perpetually transforming relationships. The visualization, a metaphorical equivalent of a state of mind,
encourages disquietude, malaise, anguish — and guilt. It underscores
the incestuous condition: two brothers and sister, beings who live
in each other's reflection — never as individuals, never growing; but
rather as stunted and dead.

> We are dead. We reached such heights of love that it made
> us want to die altogether with the loved one, and so we
> did. . . . We were never even born. We have no ordinary
> sensual life, no contact with reality. (UGB, 37)

"The glass bell covered the entire house." *Covered* and *house* are
important words. They are envelopes; protective devices, like damp
"dark caves"; each is a void, nurtures like a warm uterus; it also stifles,
paradoxically, and is death-dealing. Covered. Claustrophobic, like
dead concepts, inherited customs, imposed traditions. Motion is
stilled; feelings imprisoned. Time sequences are non-existent. An
atmosphere of disintegration, stasis, is imposed upon reader and protagonists. Time freezes. Space congeals. Yet, within this preconscious matter the instinctual domain becomes activated; and the single
creative act is fomented. Germination occurs. Subject and object
fuse in muted tones. An unsettling emotional condition comes into
being.

In Nin's secret world of analogy, the primordial vibrations of the
bell are sounded in silence, like a heaving heart. They create a visceral
response in the reader, setting up an empathetic state which is defined
as a "feeling into"; the depth of the attachment depending upon the
power of the reader's projection. Because line suggests mass and
form, and light suggests the fluidity of an emotional tone, so a phy-

sical and mental involvement in the metaphorical image is increased in *Under a Glass Bell* — just as it does in the mobiles, stabiles, and kinetic art objects of Agam, Tinguely, Calder, and Bury.

Perception for Nin — as for Paul Klee[17] — is a vital process which occurs within living matter; it is controlled instinct. It is "multi-directional" and "arbitrary"; it awakens confused sensations. Nin's visual world, as represented by the bell, the glass, and the enclosed house, is non-Euclidean. It is not representational. It does not delineate the physical space as does a Renaissance painting; rather, it brings a spiritual and emotional area to life as concretized in the statues and paintings of the Middle Ages or those of modern times. Nin has banished from the view the three-dimensional picture space which belongs to the reader's reality. Hers bathes in dimensionless tonal values, spatial planes, and transparencies — the space of a Magritte or an Ernst. Her visual image provokes a synchronistic condition. It inhabits a space/time continuum where reader and protagonists are static as well as mobile, lose footing and stand firm. The world of the mystic now comes into being; with it, a world of transcendence, the experience of *Bardo,* which Nin said she *knew* during the creative process — "that intermediate state between death and rebirth" — the voidness from which creation arises.

"The glass bell covered the entire house." A visual perception arises from this suprapersonal matrix of her collective unconscious in the form of an archetypal image. The glass, the bell, and the house do not create an inner experience; rather, an inner correspondence. Because Nin was more sensitive than the ordinary individual, she sounded out her own depths more profoundly, contacting a primordial past devoid of rational time concepts. In this inexpressible world she came to know "the obscure feelings" of the solemn and the grandiose — the world beyond appearances, the *mysterium tremendum.* It is in this penumbra that the latent energy slumbered in her soul, where the creative force first transformed itself into the archetypal image that must not be defined as an "inherited idea, but rather as an inherited mode of psychic functioning." The image of the glass bell which covered the house emerged into her consciousness; it was articulated in the body of her story; and created a kind of "magnetic field" between reader and protagonists — a veritable center of energy. It influenced, even obsessed, and deformed her vision in the process: narcissism, incest, solipsism. Nin's descent into self enabled her as an artist to confront her impulses, to perceive cataclysms, and to foresee abysses. Endowed with the magical powers of the creative individual — or with divine force — her feelings and instincts were paralleled in the visual experience.

Nin rendered the indeterminate palpable; she transformed by limiting. A visionary capable of traversing the frontiers that separate the material domain from the unmanifested and inner rhythms from a music of the spheres, she drew on unknown factors in her writings — acausal phenomena — to articulate her "forgotten memory images." D. H. Lawrence, who "restated mysticism in modern terms," and Dr. René Allendy, who taught her the occult arts and introduced her to the inner world through the therapeutic process, were her mentors. Her new states of awareness were embodied like painful and joyous litanies in *Under a Glass Bell*. A *niveau océanique* is reached in this novella with the appearance of nonverbal zones: worldless images are articulated in musical tonalities and associations; feelings are sensed in the sifting, cutting, and atomization of objects. The mystery of mood and of being is incubated in *Under a Glass Bell*, and its secrets revealed in particles, aromas, liquid experiences, layers of past sensations and energetic principles. Like a *rideau sonore*, it becomes an instrument of regeneration: alive, vibrant, and creative — enabling Nin "to reach out further mystically. . . ."

NOTES

1.   Anais Nin, *D. H Lawrence An Unprofessional Study* (London: Neville Spearman, 1961).

2.   Anais Nin, letter to Bettina Knapp, December 26, 1969 (unpublished).

3.   William James, *The Varieties of Religious Experience* (New York: New American Library, 1958), p. 293.

4.   E. D. Hirsch, Jr., "Literary Evaluation as Knowledge," in L. S. Dembo, *Criticism* (Madison: University of Wisconsin Press, 1968), p. 49.

5. Albert Einstein, *Out of My Later Years* (New York: Philosophical Library, 1950), p. 260.

6. G. S. Kirk and J. E. Raven, *The Presocratic Philosophers* (Cambridge: At the University Press, 1957), p. 196.

7. C. G. Jung, *Memories, Dreams, Reflections* (New York: Pantheon Books, 1963), p. 382.

8. Serge Hutin, *Societiées secrètes* (Paris: Presses Universitaires de France, 1970), p. 10.

9. In time Nin realized that Allendy's approach to his patients was in general ultra-scientific. His relentless probing, his reductive analyses of her dreams, reveries, and free associations, she realized, were cut and dry. He did not really "understand the artist." Allendy wanted his patients to adapt to life, to the mundane world — to be normal. Nin knew she could never resemble the masses, the crowd, nor did she want to. Her views on life were hers; and they were different from those expressed by the status quo. Her artistic temperament reacted according to its own make-up and logic.

10. Anais Nin, *Diary, I* (New York: Harcourt, Brace and World, Inc., 1966), p. 77.

11. Charles Beaudouin, Jean Desplanque, and René Jaccard, *René Allendy* (Genève: Editions du Mont-Blanc, 1945), pp. 26-27.

12. Marie Louise von Franz, *Numbers and Time* (Evanston: Northwestern University Press, 1974), pp. 204, 62, 18.

13. *Ibid.*

14. René Allendy, *Le Symbolisme des Nombres* (Paris: Bibliothèque Chacornac, 1921), p. ii.

15. Herbert Read, *Art and Alienation* (New York: The Viking Press, 1970), p. 22.

16. Anais Nin, *Under a Glass Bell* (New York: Anais Nin Press, 1958), pp. 36-37.

17. Read, *Art and Alienation*, p. 73.

Reprinted from *Research Studies*, 47, 3 (September, 1979),
published by
Hunter College and the Graduate Scenter of CUNY
New York, New York

The Dream and the Stage:
A Study of the Dream in Anais Nin's Fiction
and in Japanese Noh Drama
by Kazuko Sugisaki

In the obituary of Anais Nin I wrote for *Seishun to Dokusho* ("Young People and Reading"), I compared her fiction with Japanese Noh drama and Kado (the way of flowers):

> With rich symbolic writing screened through the filter of artistry and with subjects that take place on a level apart from everyday reality, Nin seeks to reach the ultimate goal of literary creation of art. This attitude has something in common with our traditional art, for instance, Noh which presents only the essential elements of theater on its symbolic stage and *Kado* where one morning-glory arranged in a humble vase can symbolize the total beauty of all flowers on earth.[1]

Later when I translated the title story of *Under a Glass Bell* for a magazine of poetry and criticism,[2] in an agonizing trial and error process of choosing just the right and perhaps the only Japanese word for the Nin text, the legitimacy of this comparison became confirmed in my mind.

Nin herself calls the stories in *Under a Glass Bell* "gemlike" and writes: "I would not change one word today, twenty years later."[3] These gemlike stories and Noh or *Kado* indeed share the same artistic concentration that sometimes requires an abstract symbolic form, a form like the dream.

In Anais Nin's symbolic writing one of the predominant elements is the dream. Nin uses dreams profusely in all of her fiction. Sharon Spencer, in her sensitive study of Nin's works, *Collage of Dreams*, gives examples of the purposes the dream can serve; she points out that dreams have many significances in Nin's art. The dream can be, Spencer states, a self-sustaining world of its own; the compensatory process that fills out the gaps in the conscious life; the power of revelation; the ideals seemingly unattainable in everyday reality; or it can provide archetypal patterns that are stored in the collective unconscious which people share.[4] This is a helpful analysis because it clarifies the different ways in which Nin used the dream at different times in her books and lectures. The meaning does vary depending on the context. In a study focused on Nin's use of dream, therefore, it might be necessary to define its meaning. However, the intention of this paper is not to pursue the general analysis of the dream used by Nin, but to concentrate on the study of her concept of the dream compared with the stage.

In the lyrical piece at the end of "The Voice," Nin compares the dream with a stage. In one of her most poetic passages she describes the dream as it is experienced by Djuna, one of the central characters in "The Voice." Djuna is lying down in a dark hotel room. She is aware that there are many rooms in the Hotel Chaotica, but as she closes her eyes the rooms cease to be rooms and they become the layers of being, of "all the things she was not yet."[5] The passage begins: "When I entered the dream I stepped on a stage. The lights cast on it changed hue and intensity like stage lights."[6] Then the dream is described in terms of its form, shape, motion, climate, and internal character.

The dream is "composed like a tower of layers without end," the walls of the dream are lined with "moist silk" and silence prevails in the labyrinth, but the steps are "a series of explosions." The dream, "a tower of layers," rises infinitely upward or coils downward "to the bowels of the earth." In the dream the sand "no longer concealed its desire to enmesh," the sea craves for possession and the earth yawns. The vegetation "breathes its lamentation," and animals, killed and stuffed fill the landscape of the dream. There is no time in the dream. There seems to be no gravitation, because a street lies perpendicular "between two abysses."

For such dreams Djuna waits in the night. And in such dreams a metamorphosis takes place, a metamorphosis that extends itself to everything. The daytime body of the woman disappears. Instead, there is a night body opened to the senses. The body's substance, form and texture change in the dream. It has not only blood but mercury also. The mercury runs "in all directions, swift, mordant, uncontrollable, spilling and running in star points, changing shape at each breath of desire, spilling and dispersing without separating." With a body such as this Djuna ceases to be a woman; she becomes a flower, plant, fish coral, mineral. She becomes "the loved one wholly possessed," a being who can experience "ecstasy without death." This is a metamorphosis that is possible only in dreams.

When the curtain of the theater of the dream is lifted, this being is in the center of the stage. "It was a stage surrendered to fragments, with many pieces left hanging in shreds." Because the dream is a filter the entire world is never admitted. This is the stage intended to represent life, not as an exact replica but as a symbolic image. The space of the dream is "like an enormous silence in which there was no sword of thought, no rending comments, no thread ever cut." And Djuna walks there "among symbols and silence."

In her waking life Djuna longs for this life on the stage, her dream. During the day she wanders from street to street searching for the dream:

> I would follow the avenues until the pain of being thus quartered became ecstasy and the two avenues fused together into a point of absolute sorrow. The drama was this window opening on the dual aspect of existence, on its dual face.[7]

When she finally finds the dream, she knows that she has achieved a miracle, living a life made only of eternal moments:

> . . . catching up with the dream. . . . . . To catch up, to live for a moment in unison with it, that was the miracle. The life on the stage, the life of the legend dovetailed with the daylight, and out of this marriage sparked the great birds of divinity, the eternal moments.[8]

Keeping in mind this concept of Nin's dream — the dream as a stage followed by the daylight that may enable one to live those rare eternal moments — let us turn our attention to the Noh drama of Japan.

Noh, the oldest form of drama in Japan, seeks to present not the realistic and detailed reproduction of daily life in terms of dialogue, action and setting, but employs a unique dramatic structure to express a poetic interpretation of human emotions.

The Noh stage is only eighteen feet square with its own roof within the theater building, supported by four pillars. No elaborate settings and backdrops are required; there is nothing but a stylized pine tree painted on the boards at the back of the stage. Hardly any props are used: an open framework of bamboo can represent a boat or a wagon. If a house is needed, a simple structure of four posts with a thin roof will do. A low square frame is used to represent a well with deep water. The music is created with only a flute, two hand-drums and a third drum beat by a stick. The chorus sits on the right side of the stage and narrates the story in much the same manner as in Greek drama.

The number of actors on the stage is limited, and very often the *shite* or doer dominates the entire stage. The *shite*, clad in a costume ornate in color and texture, may dance and perform alone for more than an hour at a time.

There is one particular category of Noh which I am anxious to describe. It is called *Mugen* Noh, the Noh of Dream and Illusion. This is the Noh that comes to my mind when I read Nin's fiction.

According to the reknowned modern Noh actor, Hisao Kanze (1925-1978), *Mugen* Noh is the most profound of all Noh dramas because it requires of the player extreme concentration of body and spirit "born from the psyche of nothingness." He states that "this nothingness can be achieved only by transcending one's own consciousness into something more majestic than that of the human being. The result is the most exquisite flower of all flowers."[9] Appropriately named, *Mugen* Noh has a definite quality of dream or illusion. In some *Mugen* Noh plays the entire second act takes place in the dream of the *waki* or supporting character. Let us follow a *Mugen* Noh as it is developed in one of the most typical and, according to Kanze, the most superb representations of this category, "Izutsu" (The Well Curb), written by Zeami[10] around 1420.

In Act I, a travelling priest, the *waki* or supporting character, walks onto the stage. The stage is, the priest says, a lonely village where the old remains of the Ariwara Temple still stand. At the front of the stage, a prop, a simple low, square frame with a small bunch of *susuki* (Japanese pampas grass) in one corner, represents a well curb and the bush around it.

The *waki* sits down at the side of the stage, and the *mae-shite*, the principle doer of Act I, slowly enters. She is a village woman, she explains; she is dressed in a colorful costume and wears a young woman's mask. While worshipping the soul of **Ariwara no Noarihira** in front of his grave in the temple garden she is addressed by the priest:

> Beautiful woman who worship s this old grave
> Who might you be?[11]

The *shite* answers that she is a village woman who lives nearby and comes here every dawn to tend the grave. Then she begins to narrate the old tale of Narihira and his wife, the daughter of Ki no Aritsune (her name is not known).

The source of the story is Chapter 23 of *The Tale of Ise,* compiled around the beginning of the tenth century; it is the oldest collection of tales based on poems. The hero of the tale, Ariwara no Narihira (825-880), a grandson of Emperor Heizei, is a legendary figure, a poet, famous for his flawless beauty and cultural refinement.

Once upon a time there lived a boy and a girl. Since they lived close to each other, as children they played together by the well in the garden. This was the first love each knew, and they became deeply attached to each other. But as they grew older, shyness interfered, and their meetings became fewer. Yet their hearts knew no other love. Narihira, now a handsome youth, composed a poem and sent it to the girl he loved, the daugther of Ki no Aritsune:

The well curb, by the well curb
I stood to measure my height.
Now I must stand so much taller
Having no sight of you for so long.

The girl answered with a poem:

Our hair parted in the middle
And we compared the length.
Now mine has grown long, below the shoulders
But I will wear it up only for you.[12]

They were married and their life together was happy. But soon the wife's parents died and left their daughter unprovided for. At the time a wife's family was responsible for the financial maintenance of her household; her parents' deaths meant a gradual deterioration of the young couple's standard of living. Narihira, not wanting to share a gloomy life with his wife, sought a more pleasant life. He began to visit a lady who lived in another province beyond the mountains and across a bay.

It was then socially acceptable for a nobleman to practice polygamy; so whenever the huband left to see his mistress, his wife sent him off without showing any sign of distress or jealousy, wishing him a happy journey. Her apparent nonchalance aroused suspicion in Narihira's mind. He wondered if she were receiving her own lover while he was away. One night, after leaving the house as usual, Narihira hid in the garden to keep a watchful eye on her. The wife, after a careful toilet, came out and sat in the corridor in deep thought. Then Narihira heard her voice in a poem:

When the wind blows
The white waves rise high in the sea.
Over the Tatsuta (rise) mountains in the dark of night
Alone, my husband must be crossing.

The poem into which the wife poured all her tender feelings — her love for him, her concern for him during the long night journey, her wish for his happiness — moved Narihira so much that he stopped his visits to the new lady altogether.

Because there is so little conflict between the characters in this story, one may wonder how such material can be made into a "drama." However, the dramatists who have written and performed *Mugen* Noh have been interested not so much in conflict but in bringing forth a mood, an atmosphere, enacting a tableau in which human emotions are symbolically crystallized.

After the story has been related in Act I of "Izutsu," in a highly stylized poetic language both by the principal character and by the chorus, the village woman leaves the stage. But first, she reveals her true identity to the travelling priest:

> The woman who was called "the woman of the well curb"
> Or the daughter of Ki no Aritsune,
> With shame I admit, it is I.

Then the chorus sings:

> She disappeared behind the well curb.
> She disappeared behind the well curb.

The travelling priest is left behind, wondering whether he is dreaming or awake. A villager, an actor dressed in humble clothes (with no mask) appears to tell the priest that the woman must indeed be the spirit of the daughter who died more than 500 years ago. The villager then exits, and the priest, again left alone, sings:

> The night is deepening
> The moon is clear over the old Ariwara Temple.
> Turning my sleeve over, as if to turn back the time
> And making it a temporary pillow
> I wait for the dream to come
> In my shallow sleep on the bed of moss,
> On the bed of moss.

Act II takes place entirely in the dream of the priest. Accompanied by a flute and large and small hand-drums, the *nochi-shite*, the doer of Act II, enters. The figure wears the village woman's mask of Act I, but on top of her feminine costume she also wears a man's robe and the headpiece of a court nobleman.

Because of the mask, this mysterious figure can represent both the village woman and, at the same time, the spirit of the wife in the old legend. And now this figure, by wearing clothing Narihira left behind, acquires a third personality, that of Narihira, the husband whom the spirit loved so dearly in her life on earth. The priest on the stage and the audience both realize this three-fold identity of the figure. The *shite* begins a dance which is called *Jyo no mai*, or the first slow dance; it is elegant and quiet. The *shite* sings:

> Narihira is no longer here.
> I, wearing the robe left by him, dance
> As he might.

The dance lasts almost fifteen minutes. There are no quick, exaggerated movements or mimed gestures. The arms are raised and the head is turned so slowly that the audience is almost unaware when a movement begins or when it changes. What this lone dancing figure on stage conveys is suggestiveness, an atmosphere of emotion, of the inner depth of our unconscious world.

W. B. Yeats, who once saw the dance of Michio Ito done in the style of Noh, wrote:

> . . . he was able as he rose from the floor . . . or as he threw out an arm, to recede from us into some more powerful life. Because that separation was achieved by human means alone, he receded but to inhabit, as it were, the deeps of the mind.[13]

Yeats, with his artist's insight, understood immediately the symbolic language of the Noh dance.

During this slow dance both the priest and the audience are gradually carried away from the level of everyday reality and brought into the inner world, the world of the unconscious, the world of dream. In this world emotional wishes and desires are constantly being born and dying, disappearing and reappearing; some are fulfilled, others are not.

As "the woman who waits"[14] glides through the clear moonlit climate of the unconscious, her wish to meet again the man she waits for becomes the wish of the priest, the wish of the audience, the shared wish of all sensitive observers.

When the dance ends, the moment of climax has yet to be reached. The *shite* pauses behind the well, the only object of an otherwise bare stage, and leaning slightly down over the well curb, she looks into the depth of the well. There she sees an image reflected in the water. It is the image of her eternal love:

> Shite: Vividly lifelike, the man in the remote past
> Appears in his robe and headpiece.
> No, it is not a woman.
> It is indeed a man.
> It is the image of Narihira,
> Oh, how deeply my heart yearns for him!

The music stops. The chorus is silent. There is absolute stillness on the stage. This is the moment of revelation. Chronological time suddenly ceases to flow. For a brief moment, the outer time that presides over our conscious life yields its domain to the inner time of our dream. The distinction between time and space no longer exists. The stage with this almost mythical figure in its center, transcends its previous illusion of the garden of the old temple and becomes a universal scene of a mysterious world, a dream.

In this scene, within the personality of this unearthly being created on the stage of *Mugen* Noh, a rare unity of emotion is manifested — the one who is loved and waited for is united with the other, who loves and waits. Now it is the man, then it is the woman. The *shite* sees Narihira's image reflected in the water of the well he used to stand by, but in reality, it is also she herself, her deep longing for eternal love. Her long sorrow thus becomes at last her happiness, her ecstasy. In this masked figure, man and woman are truly united into one. It seems that Zeami (1363-1443) who wrote "Izutsu" and perfected it on the stage when he was in his sixties, understood what Jung more than four hundred years later was to term "anima" and "animus," the female and the male selves we all contain within us.

Moreover, what is extraordinary about the *Mugen* Noh is that it made this moment of revelation visible and tangible to the audience, making this reality of the unconscious into a form of drama, mainly through symbols, images and brief poems. *Mugen* Noh draws the audience into an orbit where art can travel freely across the boundary between the conscious and the unconscious, between everyday reality and the dream.

Then, in the final scene, the figure slowly goes off stage and disappears as the chorus sings:

> The appearance of the dead woman's soul
> Is like a withered flower.
> Its color is lost, only the scent lingers.
> The bell of Ariwara Temple
> Tolls gently as the gentle dawn visits the old temple.
> The wind blows through the pines.
> A plaintain leaf is broken,
> And the dream is broken
> Into the awakening

The travelling priest, who has sat through the entire second act, now stands up and quietly exits. As quiet as it is, his moving body reminds the audience of the fact that there is a strong link between dream and reality.

The stage is now empty; but the song echoes. The dream is broken as the plaintain leaf is broken. Even so, the broken leaf, a concrete object, remains as if to prove that what the audience has just witnessed is not merely illusion, not merely the product of their imagination.

Perhaps I have lingered too long on "Izutsu," but I hope this description of *Mugen* Noh will help the reader understand a rather enigmatic point Zeami once made. In *Fukyo-ku-shu* he stated that one contains many, while two are just two. The single doer, the *shite*, on the almost bare stage of Noh can, as we have seen, represent not only the many aspects of delicate emotion of a man-woman, the androgyny we all possess within ourselves, but also the multiple i-dentities a single person can assume. Zeami's statement also resonates with the example of the single morning-glory of *Kado*, which I cited near the beginning of my article.

And I believe this is similar to Nin's concept of the dream as a stage. The dream is compared by Nin to a stage where only the essence of reality, of truth, is concentrated. The process of distillation, of reduction, is absolutely necessary to produce the essence, the truth unveiled and caught by the artist's creative spirit. By stripping away all the outer layers of realism, Nin sought to create the most powerful tableaux to represent her truth, emotional reality seen from inside a woman's psyche. In Nin's fiction these tableaux are abundant, but one of the most poignant was created for the novella "Stella."

A lonely figure, Stella, sits on the stairway listening for the ring of her telephone. If it rings and she yields to the temptation to answer, she risks being drawn back to her lover, Bruno, and to her suffering in an unfulfilled relationship with him. Stella is also listening to the music she deliberately plays on the phonograph. Her emotion sways between two polarities, the telephone which represents "the life with Bruno and the undertows of suffering" and the music, "emotional strength which Bruno was incapable of rivalling."[15]

Even though the scene takes place in Stella's apartment, Nin's description makes it extremely theatrical. It could very well be a stage production with one simple prop, a stairway in the center and a woman sitting on the steps. No dialogue and no actions are needed.

In an interview, Henry Miller told me that when he asked Nin where she would like to have lived, she answered immediately — Japan. I regret very much that this wish of hers did not materialize. It would have been invaluable for us, if we had had the opportunity to see Japanese culture and literature reflected by this sensitive and pene-trating artist. But this was not destined. Neither was there any specific relationship of direct influence between Anais Nin's fiction and Japanese Noh.

As far as we know, Nin saw the Noh drama only once when she
visited Japan in 1966, after she had written all of her published fiction.
There is a very brief description of the experience in her Diary (VII):

> . . . a Noh play, a profound experience in abstraction. The
> voices, as if disguised; the gestures, slow. The floor is so
> highly polished it looks like water. It is like a series of
> tableaux, or prints. Everything is suggested. The audience
> is serious, as if they were attending a mass.[16]

Unfortunately, we do not know what Noh she observed. (Could
it be *Mugen* Noh?) But certainly Nin caught some of the essential
elements the drama seeks to represent on the stage — suggestiveness,
tableaux-like images, abstraction.

I often wonder what Anais Nin would have felt, would have written,
if she could have read the texts of *Mugen* Noh or seen them performed.
Yukio Mishima wrote a modern Noh. Poems by a contemporary
woman, Chieko Takamura, were made into Noh. Someday perhaps
one of Anais Nin's novels could be written and performed as Noh
drama. After all, in the realm of art everything is possible.

NOTES

1.   "Fuho ni Yosete ("On Anais Nin's Death: An Obituary")," *Seishun
to Dokusho,* Shuei-sha, Tokyo: April, 1977, pp. 40-41.

2.   The translation appeared in *Eureka,* April, 1977, pp. 240-244.

3.   "Writing Fiction," *The Novel of the Future,* p. 85.

4.   Sharon Spencer, *Collage of Dreams* (Chicago: The Swallow Press,
1977), pp. 46-47.

5.   "The Voice," *Winter of Artifice,* p. 170.

6.   Short quotations in this section are all from "The Voice," pp. 170-
173.

7.   *Ibid.,* p. 175.

8.   *Ibid.*

9.   Kanze, Hisao, *Kokoro yori Kokoro ni Tsutauru Hana (Flowers
Conveyed from Heart to Heart: A Collection of Essays),* Hakusui-sha, Tokyo,
1979, p. 47.

10.   Zeami Motokiyo (1363-1443), actor, playwright, theorist, critic, is assumed to have written more than 100 Noh plays. He also wrote numerous essays on the art of Noh, most of which were not made public until the beginning of this century.

11.   All quotations from "Izutsu" ("The Well Curb") are translated from the original text by the author of this essay.

12.   It was the custom of high-class young women to wear their hair up only when they were married.

13.   W. B. Yeats, "Certain Noble Plays of Japan," *Essays and Introductions* (New York: MacMillan, 1961), p. 225.

14.   The *Shite* of "Izutsu" is so termed among Noh actors.

15.   "Stella," *Winter of Artifice*, p. 26.

16.   *Diary, VII*, p. 11.

Anais Nin
Sister to the Creators of Modern Dance
by Dolores Brandon

Dance may be the single art form in which it is possible to see woman's creative sensibilities as distinctively different from those of man. The dancer, like all performing artists, has little choice but to know the particularities of the body, and one's gender is an unavoidable factor in the development of a personal style. Actual gender need not dictate form. although it seems to influence it rather significantly. This is sharply apparent in both the Kabuki dance and the European ballet. In Kabuki, the dancer, always male — creates exquisitely formal female characters according to long-held notions of femininity. And despite ballet's tendency to deify woman, the discipline and form demand a complete redoing of all that is natural to the female body.

In direct contrast is modern dance — a tradition I perceive to be intensely Feminist, not just because women are the dominant creators, but also because each of its earliest choreographers develops a style and system of movement according to a very personal experiential analysis of her own body. From that analysis, an aesthetic is born, sometimes codified and passed on. In effect, the modern dancer elects, as did Nin, "to create herself in her own image."

Anais Nin is best known for her *Diaries*: eleven published volumes provide a detailed and explicit chronicle of her life and journey as an artist. Out of these undisguised personal experiences she creates a separate body of fiction. A diligent study of the *Diary* and fiction reveals an amazing reconstruction. Nin deliberately draws upon the details of herself and friends to create archetypes for modern times. It is this foundation in the personal that seems to me consistently characteristic of women's creativity. Djuna, the dancer of Nin's "continuous novel" *Cities of the Interior,* for instance, greatly resembles Nin's own public persona:

In the external world she was the woman who had sub-
mitted to mysterious outer fatalities beyond her power to
alter, and in her interior world, she was a woman who had
built many tunnels deeper down, where no one could reach
her, in which she deposited her treasures safe from destruction and in which she built a world exactly opposite of the
one she knew.

But at the moment of dancing a fusion took place, a
welding, a wholeness. The cut in the middle of her body
healed and she was all one woman dancing.

Lifted and impelled by an inner rhythm . . .[1]

This passage also illustrates three ideas to be elaborated in this
essay. One — the personal as it gets transmuted to the impersonal in
the art of a woman: two, Nin's use of dance as a recurrent motif in
character development: and, three, her belief in dance as a healing
activity, a belief that links her with a whole tradition of dancers who
were "lifted and impelled by an inner rhythm."

Beginning with Isadora Duncan (1878-1927) and ending with Pearl
Primus (1919—), I will discuss seven dancers, six American: Duncan,
Ruth St. Denis, Martha Graham, Doris Humphrey, Katherine Dunham,
and Pearl Primus; and one German, Mary Wigman. They are representatives of the earliest generations of modern dance and are indis-
putable originators; each brings a high degree of personal vision and
purpose to the art of dance. Significantly, they were all alive and
productive during Nin's lifetime (1903-1977).

This essay relies heavily on quotations from the autobiographical
and "self-critical" writings of each of the women. Because they have
left an exhaustive legacy of diaries, notes, articles, and commentaries,
it is possible to examine their work from the inside out and to draw
what I hope will be acutely human connections among them. The
possible interconnections between Nin and the modern dance world
are so myriad and multiple this article is a mere skeleton of what
could become a book-length study. The validity of female artistry
has often been disputed. Ever since Freud set forth the theory of
penis envy and woman's essential inferiority, women have had to

suffer irrational and nonsensical denials of their capacities as artists. In fact, there can be no disputing woman's unique and special contribution to dance throughout time and history. Nin absorbed and ultimately transcended the sexist elements of psychoanalysis in both her life and writings. She dedicated her journey to the exploration and expression of the Feminine. And with more or less individual consciousness, each dancer included here chose to break the same taboos. Each entered the "Feminine" armed with passion as well as intellect.

Women may have dominated the ballet stages of the Romantic Age in Europe. However, men were the theorists, choreographers, and managers. The ballet never took hold in America (nor, interestingly, since Wigman is the only European dancer to be considered here, in Germany). Americans regarded ballet as outmoded fantasy with nothing to say to the pioneers of a new world. It was the art of the world Americans had escaped. As the twentieth century dawned an antitraditional spirit asserted itself throughout the Western world. Women demanded the vote. The work of Freud (born in 1856) and of Jung (1878) began to affect the ways men and women defined themselves.

> In the 1880's a continent apart, two little girls who were destined to alter the course of dance, of theater, of art itself, were dancing with nature. Isadora [Duncan] by the ocean in California; Ruthie [St. Denis] by the fields and streams of the old farm [Pin Oaks, New Jersey]. They did more than imitate nature in dance — that was a way of dance as old as man himself — they let nature invade their spirits and in it they found faith as well as art.[2]

In the simple acts of removing their shoes, dancing with their bare feet on the earth; exchanging the corset and stays of ballet artifice for soft shapeless tunics, they reclaimed and named themselves.

Nin chose sandals and noticed herself dressing more simply as "analysis" permitted her to be herself. To go forward they journey back to find mythologies in which "the Feminine" is the equal of the Masculine. Duncan says "the dance of the future will have to become a religious high art as it was for the Greeks. For art which is not religion is not art, is mere merchandise."[3]

She looks to the future when women "will dance not in the form of the nymph, nor fairy, nor coquette, but in the form of woman in her greatest and purest expression." Woman, Isadora asserts, "will realize the mission of the woman's body and the holiness of its parts."[4]

Ruth St. Denis restored "to dance in America what India, Japan, China and most of the rest of the world expected — that the dancing body represent life on a higher plane."[5] She sought and found identity and art in the great Oriental mythologies. As much poet and mystic as dancer, she said of herself in full seriousness:

> I am Kwan Yin, the Merciful, the Compassionate. All men and women, and children and all beasts, and all creeping creatures and all flying things receive my Love.
> For I am Kwan Yin, the Mother Merciful, who hears and answers prayers.[6]

Interestingly, as the rhythms of the Machine Age intensified, literally everyone began to dance. Both popular and serious dance expressions evoked the primitive, the ancient. This did not surprise Mary Wigman (1886-1973) who wrote, "our technical age brings forth the dancer. If we consider that behind the machine stands the primeval force of rhythm, that every machine represents a tamed rythmic force . . . we can . . . say of our age today that its distinguishing feature is its rhytmic feeling."[7]

In 1939 Martha Graham said:

> America's greatest gift to the arts is rhythm: rich, full, unabashed, virile. Our two forms of indigenous dance, the Negro and the Indian, are as dramatically contrasted rhythmically as the land in which they root . . . though they may be basically foreign to us . . . they are akin to the forces that are at work in our life . . . for we as a nation are primitive also . . . primitive in the sense that we are forming

a new culture . . . a new fabric . . . from the threads of many
old cultures. . . ."[8]

Almost all of Nin's women characters are "primitive" in Graham's
sense; Nin forms new women from the threads of old roles. She takes
her own life, her body, she challenges all that is said to be woman's
"place," woman's nature. Nin observes herself and others closely as
if in a laboratory, and gives back a portrait of twentieth century
woman. It is a woman in motion: "Her mobility was now her only
defense against new dangers. While you are in movement, it is harder
to be shot at, to be wounded even."[9]

In an essay entitled "The Dance of Life" Havelock Ellis wrote:

> . . . the art of dancing stands at the source of all the arts
> that express themselves first in the human person. . . . If
> we are indifferent to the art of dancing, we have failed to
> understand, not merely the supreme manifestation of physi-
> cal life, but also the supreme symbol of spiritual life. . . .
> Dancing is the primitive expression alike of religion and love
> — of religion from the earliest human times we know of and
> of love from a period long anterior to the coming of man.[10]

Love is the nectar of both sacred and secular longing. In the realm
of religious practice we in the West have inherited, love excludes
the sensual and erotic. Sex is either to be avoided altogether or to
be used solely for the purpose of procreation. Birth is understood
within a context of original sin. Dancing — once an integral part of
sacred ritual, even in the Christian church — is no longer permitted
by the Western religions formed primarily by the intellect. These
are the religions of patriarchy, religions that exclude woman, deeming
her "untouchable." To dance is to embrace, to include, to accept
"the Feminine." As dance was banned from the church, it became
less and less acceptable except as it served the courtship rites that
led to marriage. Generally, "polite" society regarded dance as a
taboo profession for either men or women. Nin well knew the subtle
way in which this rejection takes place. In *Winter of Artifice*, Djuna,

a dancer, recognizes her father's opposition to her art:

> Once she was dancing on the stage. . . . The Spanish music
> carried her away, whirled her into a state of delirium. . . .
> Her eyes fell on the front row. She saw her father there.
> He was holding a program before his face in order not to
> be recognized. But she knew his hair, his brow, his eyes. It
> was her father. Her steps faltered, she lost her rhythm.
> Only for a moment. Then she swung around, stamping her
> feet, dancing wildly and never looking his way until the end.
> When she saw her father years later she asked him if he
> had been there. He answered that not only was he not
> there but that if he had the power he would have prevented
> her from dancing because he did not want his daughter
> on the stage. . . .
> As soon as she left him everything began to sing again.
> . . . Her father was the musican, but in life he arrested
> music. . . .
> As soon as she left her father she heard music again.
> . . . It was her faith in the world which danced again.[11]

Coincidentally perhaps, almost all the dancers discussed here had a
repressive relationship with their fathers. In no case did a father
actively encourage or support his daughter's passion for dance. In
almost every case, the mother defied the opposition or indifference
of the father and encouraged her daughter's flowering.

Isadora never really knew her father. Her mother had divorced
him when she was "a baby in arms." But, she writes:

> All my childhood seemed to be under the black shadow of
> this mysterious father of whom no one would speak, and
> the terrible word divorce was imprinted on the sensitive
> plate of my mind. . . . In George Eliot's *Adam Bede* there
> is a little girl who does not marry, a child that comes un-
> wanted, and the terrible disgrace which falls upon the poor
> mother. I was deeply impressed by the injustice of this state

of things for women, and putting it together with the story
of my father and mother, I decided, then and there, that I
would live to fight against marriage and for the emancipation of women and for the right for every woman to have
a child or children as it pleased her. . . .[12]

Her own mother had so enthusiastically and courageously lived
out motherhood, it is not surprising that Isadora bore two children.
Even after she had given birth to her first child, Deirdre, and could
recall the ecstasy and power of that moment, when confronted with
the fact of a second pregnancy, Isadora tells how she was filled "with
revolt that such a deformation should again come to [her] body,
which was the instrument of [her] art." In the midst of her horror
a transformation occurred: ". . . again tortured by the call, the hope,
the vision of that angel's face, the face of my son . . . Finally, I rose
and spoke. . . . No, you shall not trouble me. I believe in Life, in
Love, in the sanctity of Nature's Law."[13] So powerful was this belief, so deep her commitment to women's freedom, she danced while
noticeably pregnant.

At nineteen Nin married Hugh Guiler. She entered that union
on the wings of song:

> I stand with arms outstretched, pleading with Life: "Oh,
> flow not so swiftly, bear me not away before I may under-
> stand what is happening to me!"
>
> Heedless of my supplications, Life flows on. I see the
> approaching month looming on the horizon, heavy with
> mysterious significance. I am at once awed and thrilled.
>
> My love is coming to me, and our marriage time is ap-
> proaching, and all this will seal the beginning of my New
> Life.
>
> No longer shall you know me as Child Heart or Dreamer
> Girl or the frail and wavering Nature, bowing beneath the
> weight of experience, but as Young Woman, Hugo's wife-to-
> be, preparing to enter the Kingdom of Kingdoms and to
> fulfill her earthly mission.[14]

Later, in the same Diary Nin describes how she and a woman friend cried together at a film about man's infidelity. She chides their sentimentality, writing, "About husbands, then, all women are sentimental and all women are fools, as far as I can see."[15]

Although Nin spent her entire adult life married, this is not at all clear to readers of the first published series, Volumes I through VII. When in 1966 the Diary began to be published, Hugh Guiler (Ian Hugo) and others asked that the details of their relationships with her be suppressed. Thus, to protect others she adopted a style which obscures the exact nature of her relationships with men. This editorial practice was abandoned when the four volumes of the "Early" Diary began to be published, starting with *Linotte* in 1978. Reading the Diaries retrospectively, then, the reader learns many details that are missing from the volumes covering the years, 1927-1974.

The first of the four "Early Diaries," does prepare us for Nin's position on motherhood. Though written to her father, this volume is, in fact, a long love letter to her mother and is the only "in depth" portrait of a traditional mother Nin ever wrote (judging from the edited *Diaries*). This mother is loved but feared as a role model, for to be mother is not to be artist/father. Nin was ultimately unable to carry a foetus to term due to a childhood operation. But she does conceive a child. We, as readers of the *Diary,* never know who the father is; we are not certain with whom she is having an affair; we do not know that she is married. We do know that she is terrified and actually prays that the child not be born: "Will you go about, as I did, knocking on windows, watching every caress and protective love given to other children? For as soon as you will be born, as just as soon as I was born, man the husband, lover, friend, will leave as my father did."[16]

It would be unfair to make this passage represent Nin's definitive statement about biological motherhood. Fate denied her children but she always assumed an intensely maternal and nurturing role in the lives of many, many artists. Certainly, in the moment of giving birth to her still-born daughter, Nin directly confronted her womanhood: "I had come upon the infinite, through the flesh and through the blood. Through flesh and blood and love, I was made whole.

I cannot say more. . . . But from that moment on, I felt my connection with God, an isolated, wordless, individual, full connection which gives me immense joy and a sense of the greatness of life, eternity. I was born. I was woman."[17] This is the last time she defined herself in this way. Thereafter, psychoanalysis and the consequent listening to the unconscious replace God in the Diaries, becoming the key links in a personal acceptance of her own divinity. Speaking for her sisters as well as for herself, she says: "Art is our only proof of continuity in a life of the spirit. When we deny it (as we have en masse and massively), we lose all that gives us a noble concept of human beings."[18]

It is is a given that one cannot exist apart from the other, and a work of art succeeds or fails in the degree to which the form and content are complementary. Although the following quotation is from Nin's *Diary* — again — it might have been expressed by every choreographer in this study: "Form is not a matter of prefabrication. . . . For me it is an inner eruption, very similar to that created by the earth itself in its perpetual evolutions. They happen according to inner tensions, inner pressures, inner accidents of climate, and it is the accumulation of such organic incidents which created mountains and oceans. To discover my own form I have first to dig very deeply into this natural source of creation."[19] Nin made this statement fairly late in her career, long after she had established the forms for which she is most remembered. It was true; her forms were not prefabricated. She began the Diary at the age of eleven, quite unselfconsciously, with the naive and poignant wish that sending it to him would hasten her father's return to the family. Or if not his actual return, that it would serve to maintain the strong spiritual bond she felt with him. Her fiction emerged as she dug "deeply into this natural source of creation."

Of her own art, Isadora wrtoe: "If people ask me when I began to dance, I reply — in my mother's womb, probably as a result of the oysters and champagne — the food of Aphrodite."[20]

In fact her learning was a little more usual than that for we know she studied dance much in the same way other young girls of the time did. The theories of Francois Delsarte (1811-1871) were much in vogue and influenced this whole group of dancers. He had been a singer at the Paris Opera, an artist who lost his voice because of bad training and who turned to studies of the relationship of anatomy and emotion.[21] He developed a detailed system of gesture. He "observed the movements of prisoners, of mothers as distinct from nursemaid, of soldiers. . . , he watched pain and ecstasy, despair and exaltation. He then evolved a theory whereby the actor could . . . project with honesty, inner feelings.[22] It was quite common for young girls to be trained in the arts of self-expression and Delsarte was part of every teacher's vocabulary. Isadora even spent time in ballet classes. But for the sake of our concern with Feminine myth-making and the delight we have in the autobiographic writings of these women, it is more important that her story be told from her point of view.

> I was born under the star of Aphrodite. . . . My life and
> my art were born of the sea. . . I have to be thankful that
> when I was young my mother was poor . . . mother was
> a musician and taught music for a living . . . she was away
> from home all day and many evenings. . . . I could wander
> alone by the sea and follow my own fantasies. . . My mother
> was too busy to think of any dangers which might befall
> her children . . . it is certainly to this wild, untrammelled
> life of my childhood that I owe the inspiration of the dance
> I created, which was the expression of freedom.[23]

St. Denis had been searching a long time for the shape of her art. Like Duncan and Nin, her precocity found early focus. Deeply spiritual by nature, she was not content with religious dogma or creed. As a child she would "emulate the Crucifixion in the secrecy of her room in order to find a physical identity with an event which had re-channeled the rush of history itself . . . She made obeisance to the sun as it set . . . It was clear to her that Jesus Christ was closer to that sun, to the sea, to all of nature than He was to the Church services she abhorred."[24] Three books read in pre-adolescent days set the stage — Mary Baker Eddy's *Science and Health With Key to the Scriptures,* Kant's *Critique of Pure Reason,* and Dumas' *Camille.* But from the day she laid eyes on a poster advertising Egyptian Deities, a brand of Turkish cigarettes, St. Denis' life direction was clear. The advertiser had chosen to entice customers with Isis, the Mother goddess of ancient Egypt, enthroned in a temple — "serene, contemplative, regal, mysterious" — amidst a pond of lotus blossoms. The effect of this poster "represented a complete break" for Miss Ruth. She began to imagine a dance in which "she intended to be Egypt herself, an entire nation as it lived the span of a day from dawn to dusk and from birth to death."[25]

St. Denis was less a dancer than an incarnation of the archetypal Feminine, the principle of the Receptive, whose main attribute is devotion. She does not combat the Creative but completes it."[26]

The first generation gave birth to the artist orginators who trained a group of dancers in their own particular style and philosophy. Both Martha Graham (born in 1894) and Doris Humphrey (1895-1958) were important students and performers with Denishawn. At around the age of thirty they left to pursue their own careers. Mary Wigman (1886-1973), working in Europe, was relatively unaware of the activities of her contemporaries in the United States, yet her course was markedly synchronous with theirs. In general, the second generation paid little homage to the recent past. They are the "virgins" of dance and insisted on defining their own maturity. The dance forms they created were as personal and idiosyncratic as those of Duncan and St. Denis, for their successors also defined dance according to their own physical knowledge of human "being." As Mary Wigman said: "We dance the constant change of mental conditions as they are alive in woman as a rhythmic flow. Let us listen to the pulse beat of our own heart, to the whisper and murmur of our own blood, which is the sound of this space. This sound wants to become song."[28]

Mary Wigman was not the prodigy Duncan, St. Denis, or Nin had been. She began to dance at the age of twenty-seven. Although she had studied with Dalcroze and was on the verge of becoming a teacher of his method, it was only when she met Laban that she really began to dance. While Dalcroze was concerned with the relationships of musical rhythm to body rhythm, Laban reduced dance to an exploration of physical rhythms, the ebb and flow of muscular impulse, tension and relaxation. He was the theorist and Wigman "was the first victim to help prove his theoretical findings . . . It was hard work for me," she wrote: "Every movement had to be done over and over again until it was controlled and could be analyzed, transposed and transformed into an adequate symbol."[29] Together they developed what came to be known as "absolute dance." The combination of Laban's rigid discipline and Wigman's deeply emotional approach produced a dance of great power and importance. It was quite different from that which Wigman's sisters developed in America. Hanya Holm, an accomplished American disciple of Wigman, articulated the difference:

> Emotionally the German [Wigman] dance is basically subjective and the American [Graham, Humphrey] dance objective in their line and characteristic manifestations . . . The tendency of the American dancer is to observe, portray and comment on her surroundings with an insight lighted mainly by an intellectual comprehension and analysis . . . The German dancer on the other hand, starts with the ritual emotional experience itself and its effect upon the individual . . . ."[30]

Wigman had to explain and defend the emotional intensity of her work in much the same way Nin (and women artists in general) had to do: "The dance, like every artistic language, takes for granted a higher or intensified feeling. And — let us not be deceived — this intensified feeling has not always a happy background. Suffering, pain, even terror and fear, can bring about an acceleration of feeling and thus of the whole being of man."[31]

It may be Nin's Cuban and European origins that allow her to stand somewhere between the European and the American, but there is something very like Wigman in her expression. *Linotte* (*The Early Diary: 1914-1920*) begins with the ritual emotional experience of losing the father. The Diary was the means by which she, "the abandoned," reconciled herself with the "abandoner." By the time Nin married and began to unravel the patterns of behavior created because of this trauma, the Diary had become a "workshop" in which she analyzed her "womanhood" and from which, as I have said before, she created her fiction. Lillian, the main character in *Seduction of the Minotaur,* the last volume in *Cities of the Interior,* is, according to Nin, her only "completely fictional woman." If Djuna seems the closest to Nin's public persona, Lillian may, in fact, represent the "real" Nin with all masks removed.

Although Lillian is not Nin's freest woman, she is, I think, the most complex. She is at once mother, mistress and artist; both faithful and faithless; masculine and feminine; heterosexual and lesbian; dependent and independent; modern and archaic; "negress" and Celt. She is the mid-twentieth century woman feverish in her quest for a new identity; a woman who "had first seen herself through her mother's eyes." She rebels: "If this is woman . . . I do not want to be one." Yet "at the same time she [feels] despair because she was as she was, and unable to be like HER, she would never be loved."[32] This despair, Nin's despair, is fundamental to all Nin's women. But:

> Lillian was journeying homeward. The detours of the labyrinth did not expose disillusion, but *unexplored dimensions.* Archaeologists of the soul never returned empty handed. Lillian had felt the existence of the labyrinth beneath her feet like the excavated passageways under Mexico City, but she had feared entering it and meeting the Minotaur who would devour her.
>
> Yet now that she had come face to face with it, the Minotaur resembled someone she knew. It was not a monster. It was a reflection upon a mirror, a masked woman, Lillian herself, the hidden masked part of herself unknown to her, who had ruled her acts. She extends her hand toward this tyrant who could no longer harm her. It lay upon the mirror of the plane's round portholes, traveling through the clouds, a fleeting face, her own, clear and definite only when darkness came."[33]

So Lillian learns (and I suspect Nin did as well) what Djuna learned:

> Henceforth she possessed this power: whatever emotion
> would ravish or torment her, she could bring it before a
> mirror, look at it, and separate herself from it. And she
> thought she had found a way to master sorrow.[34]

Wigman finds the same power in dance. It is more difficult to report on, however, for once the curtain falls the dance is gone. Fortunately photographs permit some tangible evidence of her expression and she leaves behind, as do all the women, exquisite memoirs, recollections and commentaries on her work. Looking at photographs of her dancing or even posing for a personal photo, we are faced with a woman we know has suffered the sorrows of an Age. She creeps and crawls against the earth, her body wholly without resistence, open to the expression of every human emotion. The impact of the photos are like no others; the emotional intensity, the aliveness of herself and the space that she "touches" — she is a living manifestation of sacred archaic sculpture. It is as if she communed with the spirits that inhabited those ancient wooden forms and now they inhabit her. She will exorcise the Evil of her time. There is not a hint of pretension or self-involvement, only pure egoless compassion:

> I was,
> I am,
> I will be,
> before you,
> with you,
> after you,
> imperishable.
>
> from *Seven Dances of Life*[35]

She starts with the feeling in herself and "the passionate desire arises . . . at the moment of execution, to become one with these dances, to disappear in them, to live them."[36] The sacred, mystic element is present as it was in the work of St. Denis but it is a mysticism born of an "atonement" with Man not God as it is in Nin. The ecstatic is not attributed to a connection with an outside force; it is perfectly within the possibility of the individual. "Without ecstasy there is no dance. Without form there is no dance."[37]

Only one of the dancers included here was ever actully mentioned by Nin — Martha Graham. Acknowledging Graham's influence on her, Nin wrote ". . . in *Ladders to Fire* I found a new way to deal with neurotic vision. . . . I fused symbols and externals. I was inspired by the dance style of Martha Graham. The placing of the characters, the symbolic enacting, the suggestiveness."[38] In a curious way, I see Graham as a kind of mirror opposite of Nin. The center of their hearts and their work is the element of dramatic conflict. Nin was and Graham is still possessed by a desire to give and receive love: Nin more obviously in her life, Graham more obviously in her work.

Of her own work Nin wrote:

> Contemplating fiction again. What happens if I leave myself out completely? Then everyone will be restored to his natural size, not mythical, not expanded, not symbolic. With me absent, and only the other characters present, I shall depict a world, with other dimensions missing, I seem to be the conductor for an expanded vision. But my alchemy poetizes them all, translates them into myth. . . .
>
> Me absent, say, from the diary, and the fire crucible is gone in which all the lives melt and combine and produce another life. I am the alchemist, not the ego."[39]

And of Graham, someone else wrote:

> . . . most central characters are surrounded by other figures, seen in low relief . . . we see these creatures as she does — through the lens of her emotional insight. They are personifications of her memories, fears, wishes, frustrations. They may be forces from without, that move in upon her — upon us. Or they may be forces from within.

> Out of the essential nature of these "characters" then
> comes conflict . . . when the two loves in *Deaths and En-
> trances* engage in an exciting fight, it is not two jealous
> men; it is two elements of love — possessive love (Dark
> Beloved); tender, transfigured love (The Poetic Beloved).
> And they are not contesting for the woman of the drama.
> They battle *within* her heart.[40]

We are never sure if what Graham dances on stage has anything to
do with what she lives. Next to nothing is known about her private
life. Her *Notebooks* tell us little of her personality, but are fascinating proof of a prodigious intellect, wholly transmuted in the "cru-
cible" of her body: fragments of legend, prayer, philosophy, fable,
history, myth and literature are therein transformed. That which in
itself is "exalted" she physically absorbs and returns as dance.

Nin's fragments are more transparently personal. She cannot imagine
it otherwise. She takes the physical and makes it WORD; "When
words and feelings learn to float they reach the poetic 'mouvement
perpetuel.' To float means to be joined to some universal rhythm."[41]
To "melt" the dancer/alchemist must surrender mind over body."
When the mind and body act in concert, we transcend the potential
tyranny of either. I think Nin employed the dance as a symbol of
integrated human expression. She recognized its healing grace, and the
couple dance is a metaphor for her belief: "The world today is root-
less; it's like a forest with all the trees with their heads in the ground
and their roots gesticulating wildly in the air, withering. The only
remedy is to begin a world of two; in two there is hope of perfection,
and that in turn may spread to all. . . . But it must begin at the base,
in relationship of man and woman."[42]

Nin's needs and means were, of necessity, somewhat different
from those of the dancers. Because her themes, like theirs, are consistently concerned with relationships, and most often with love relationships between men and women, the popular couple dances of
her day offered images as important to the world she created as the
"ballets of Martha Graham." The words "waltz," "mambo" and
"jazz" permit a reader ready entry to Nin's fiction. Her use of dance

can be seen as a Rorschach test of a character's class, temperament and style. Time and again it is a major means through which Nin delineates character.

How the individual choreographers dance in relation to their group and how they direct other dancers to move in relation to each other is a major distinguishing feature of these second generation women. Doris Humphrey seems to have been the first to create a group dance in which she herself was accepted as an intrinsic part of the total expression. This may be as attributable to her skills as a teacher as to her gifts as a dancer, choreographer and theorist. She believed one could stimulate feeling through design and that it was easier to perceive design with a group than with a single figure. Because she was so committed to the shaping of groups into patterns of rhythm, Humphrey is the only one of the group to be critically hailed as a choreographer. Like Wigman she composed without music and experimented with the dancer's voice as a source of accompaniment. *Water Study*, composed in 1927, was a silent dance in which the dancer's breathing was intended to be heard; this breathing coupled with the pounding of the dancers' bare feet and the rustling of their movements became the breath, pulse, and rustling of the waves their arching backs and plunging bodies resembled. Humphrey built the dance on the rise and fall, in angled curves, and dressed the dancers in flesh-colored leotards to effect an abstraction of the bodies within a mood created by blue lights. It was "pure" dance. "The language of dance," she wrote, "is mood. Mood is where dance lives."[43] Later, in "Life of the Bee" Humphrey used a chorus of humming voices, humming through tissue paper-covered combs as the only accompaniment. She, too, glimpsed her own "mouvement perpetuel" when she selected Mother Anne Lee and the Shaking Quakers as material for her masterpiece, "The Chosen," later known as "The Shakers." In the singing and dancing ecstasies of this Christian American sect, Humphrey found tangible and translatable evidence of her own theories. "She saw man's impulse toward progress, his ambitious drive, versus his desire for stability and peace as the excitement of movement and the exhilarating danger of fall. Humanity exists in an area of spiritual conflict . . . from which it alternately moves in 'an arc between two deaths' — that of equilibrium or exalted quietude and one of submission to an opposing force."[44] It seems to me," she said, "that the motivation behind all my dances from "The Shakers" to the "Choral Preludes" (fifteen years) has been the same to the point of monotony — and can be epitomized in the Shaker faith that 'ye shall be saved when ye are shaken free of sin.'"[45]

As Isadora had predicted, America raised the dance "to the most noble of all arts." She had described "America dancing, standing with one foot poised on the highest point of the Rockies, her two hands stretched out from the Atlantic to the Pacific . . . her forehead shining with the Crown of a million stars."[46] "A necessary part of that development," Graham said, "was that we became aware of the ground on which we have been bred physically and psychically."[47] That ground has been trod by the feet of all humankind — men and women, Black, Red and White. It is the ground Nin traveled in "a Ford Model A with the top down." A trip to the West delivered her of the toxins of New York and gave her a "taste for nature, for people who were natural and gracious."

If I had not traveled West," she wrote, "I might not have wanted to become a permanent resident."[48]

It was in the South where Pearl Primus "in 1944 discovered in the Baptist churches the voice of the drum — in the throat of the preacher. I found the dynamic sweep of movement through space . . . in the motions of the minister and congregation alike. I felt in the sermons the crashing thunder dances of Africa and I was hypnotized by the pounding rhythm of song."[49] And it was in the Middle Western city of St. Louis where young Katherine Dunham recalled that "there began a possession by the blues . . . deeper than prayer and closer to the meaning of life than anything else . . . something people are supposed to know about and don't look at, or knew a long time ago and lost."[50] For these two Black women, dance was as much a means through which they, like other women, defined themselves "in their own image," and it was also a way of obtaining for their race "a permanent and dignified recognition." Both Blacks and women, in spite of their considerable contributions to the United States and the world, are feared, suspected of being closer to the "primitive." This association can be either positive or negative, depending on who's making it and for what purposes. Characteristically, Nin knew that "the primitive and the poet never parted company. Intellectual knowledge is not enough. Music, the dance, poetry and painting are the channels for emotions. It is through them that experience penetrates our bloodstream. Ideas do not."[51]

We are all too familiar with the myopic and inhumane elements of Western society who concede genius to Blacks only in their ability to dance and sing. Dunham insists that all primitive peoples dance, the Negro no more ably than any other:

> It is merely that all primitives solve their psychological difficulties most easily in motor activities — often in a form of exhibitionism. Thus, because of the minority position of the Negro here, we unfortunately are apt to become exhibitionists. And since a carry over of our native rhythm has become a part of our tradition, obviously expected of us, we dance a lot. It's a healthy release mechanism, but I don't agree that it is a more natural medium of racial expression.[57]

And Primus reminds us: "The first responsibility of everyone is to be human. That is the underlying trait of all people and, I hope, of my dancing. If you put up a fence in your mind with *Negro* on it, you are guilty of intellectual segregation."[53]

"To be human," yes. It seems so simple. Yet as nature becomes more apparently within the control of man, people become less valuable to each other. As we advance technologically, these "intellectual segregations" become more and more acceptable. Technological advance comes at a heavy price. Carl Jung was among the first to warn of the consequences: "Civilized life today demands concentrated, directed conscious functioning, and this entails the risk of a considerable dissociation from the unconscious. The further we are able to remove ourselves from the unconscious through directed functioning, the more readily a powerful counterposition can build up in the unconscious, and when this breaks out it may have

disagreeable consequences."[54]   To avoid these "disagreeable consequences" we need a synthesis. "We need the unconscious contents
to supplement the conscious attitude."[55] In the twentieth century
the artist is the best equipped person to integrate the unconscious
with the conscious, because he or she knows how to give form to
dream.

In all my books," Nin wrote, "There is a return to the dream, the
source of mystery, where the character seeks the key to its own meaning."[56] Graham "wanted to go back through the motor memory to
the ancestral moods to find an explanation of what we are today."
"She came to the conclusion that mythology was the psychology of
another age. . . . She uses the symbols of mythology as ancestors of
present day moods."[58]

Both Dunham and Primus "lived too long with people who do not
believe in magic."[59] As anthropologists they traveled to the Carib-
bean and Africa where "people still use their bodies as instruments
through which every conceivable emotion or event is projected. The
result is a strange but hypnotic marriage between life and dance. The
two are inseparable. No child could be born, no man buried without
dance."[60] In the dance rituals of the African peoples these women
witnessed first-hand the wedding of form and function. For them,
no special measures are required to bring up the unconscious. Both
Dunham and Primus used social science to return to the very sources
of art.

Intuitively, all of the women discussed here sought in dance rituals
of self-healing. Katherine Dunham found in the ritual dances of the
Dahomey, a Haitian Voudoun cult, not only the inspiration for her
art but also a belief system which she, to this day, practices. She
describes how, in 1977, she experienced the second of five "fire"
baptisms:

> I have a feeling if I go into it deeply and sincerely, I
> will meet myself coming around the other way. I'll know
> more about dance, more about what I haven't been able to
> express. I feel that if I can master it as the Haitian Vodoun
> have mastered it, I will find a beauty that is far beyond

what I've experienced of beauty otherwise. I am finding
this higher beauty, and it's what I want."[61]

Dunham could say this with full confidence, for her experience of
beauty enhanced the lives of so many people. Equally comfortable
in film, theater, and opera, Dunham's output is enormous. It is not
easy to translate an eight-day ceremony into eight minutes and have
it move those who think they are merely seeking entertainment. But
Dunham achieved this when she presented "Rites of Passage" in 1941
at Yale University. Subtitled "An Anthropological Approach to
Theater," "Rites of Passage" dealt with two crises in human life:
the reaching of adolescence and the search for a mate. This work was
so powerful, so profound that it was banned by the Boston "brah-
mins." Dunham taught people their own history and invited them to
pick up the modern-day threads of their ancient past.

Of herself Dunham wrote: "I am not a dancer. I am not an an-
thropologist. I am an evangelist."[62] She preaches the joy of life
and the beauty of her people, choosing to develop a technique that
was as important to the white world as to the black. "She strove
to develop a system of primitive pattern that could be as substan-
tially articulate as anything, either modern or classical."[63] At her
school in New York (in the same studio that Isadora once used),
students can study primitive rhythm, percussion, dance history, an-
thropology, and even ballet. Similarly, Primus prepared a Ph.D. thesis
on "African Sculpture: Its Function in Society." Taking basic pos-
tures from African sculpture, she created a dance which grew from
sculpted forms. Years later, during World War II, she composed "Our
Spring Will Come," a dance dedicated to the Europeans and Asians
who were helping refugees; in unity, Primus taught, there is strength
and freedom.

Duncan, St. Denis, Wigman, Graham, Humphrey, Dunham, Primus,
and Nin — all chose the body as an instrument through which the
"whole tribe" could speak. Nin received thousands of letters from
women saying, "You've written my story. Thank you."

A consistent humane and compassionate approach to life marks
the work of each of these artists. As personal as their work often is,

it can never be labeled "egocentric." The personal is merely the most available access point to their understanding. Possibly because woman's relationship to her body is so much more private and intimate, she has a deeper knowledge of its riches and reveals these treasures with more solemnity and reverence. When woman chooses to "speak" with and through her body, she begins to create a "world exactly opposite of the one she knew."[64]

NOTES

1.   Anais Nin, *Cities of the Interior* (Chicago: Swallow, 1959), pp. 131-132.

2.   Walter Terry, *Miss Ruth — The More Living Life of Ruth St. Denis* (New York: Dodd, Mead & Co., 1969), p. 5.

3.   Isadora Duncan, "The Dance of the Future," *Women in Theater — Compassion and Hope* (New York: Drama Book Publishers, 1983), p. 108.

4.   Nancy L Ruyter, *Performers and Visionaries — The Americanization of the Art of Dance* (New York: Dance Horizon, 1979), p. 45.

5.   *Miss Ruth,* p. 52.

6.   Christina Schlund, *Into the Mystic with Miss Ruth* (New York: Dance Perspectives, 1971), p. 27.

7.   *The Mary Wigman Book* (Middletown, Connecticut: Wesleyan University Press, 1973), p. 143.

8.   Merle Armitage, *Martha Graham — The Early Years* (New York: Da Capo, 1978), p. 99.

9.   *Cities of the Interior,* p. 335.

10.   *Dance Anthology,* ed. Cobbett Steinberg (New York: New American Library, 1980), pp. 238-239.

11.   Anais Nin, *Winter of Artifice — Three Novelettes* (Chicago: 1948), pp. 98-99.

12.   Isadora Duncan, *Isadora — My Life* (Garden City, New York, 1927), pp. 16-17.

13.   *Isadora,* p. 240.

14.   Anais Nin, *The Early Diary of Anais Nin — Volume II — 1920-1923* (New York: Harcourt Brace Jovanovich, 1982), p. 522.

15.   *Anais — An International Journal,* Volume I, p. 40.

16.   Anais Nin, *The Diary, Volume I — 1931-1934* (New York: Harcourt Brace Jovanovich, 1966), p. 339.

17.   The Diary, I, p. 348.

17. *The Diary*, I, p. 348.
18. *The Diary*, V, p. 191.
19. *The Diary*, IV, pp. 152-153.
20. *Isadora*, p. 9.
21. *Miss Ruth*, p. 7.
22. *Miss Ruth*, pp. 8-9.
23. *Isadora*, pp. 10-11.
24. *Miss Ruth*, pp. 4-5.
25. *Miss Ruth*, p. 41.
26. *I Ching* (Princeton, New Jersey: Princeton University Press, 1970), p. 10.
27. Denishawn was the name given to the school and company of dance established by Ruth St. Denis and her husband, Ted Shawn.
28. "Mary Wigman and Martha Graham: Dance in Counterpoint", a manuscript by Beverly Cassia Brown. The Dance Collection of the Lincoln Center Library for the Performing Arts, New York, p. 6.
29. *The Mary Wigman Book*, p. 39.
30. *The Mary Wigman Book*, p. 160.
31. *The Mary Wigman Book*, p. 142.
32. Anais Nin, *Seduction of the Minotaur* (Chicago: Swallow, 1972), p. 84.
33. *Seduction of the Minotaur*, p. 111.
34. *Cities of the Interior*, p. 138.
35. *The Mary Wigman Book* p. 79.
36. Paul Love, *Modern Dance Terminology* (Kamin Dance Publishers, 1953, p. 34.
37. Walter Sorrell, *Dance Through the Ages* (New York: Grossett and Dunlap, 1967), p. 185.
38. *The Diary*, IV, p. 120.
39. *The Diary*, III, pp. 293-294.
40. From a progam book in Beatrice Hellebrandt's Scrapbooks, 1928 — 50 — Dance Collection, Lincoln Center Library for the Performing Arts.
41. *The Diary*, II, p. 128.
42. *Cities of the Interior*, p. 337.
43. Margaret Lloyd, *The Borzoi Book of Modern Dance* (New York: Knopf, 1949), p. 87.
44. Olga Maynard, *American Modern Dancers: The Pioneers* (Toronto: Little, Brown, & Co., 1965), p. 131.
45. Selma Jeanne Cohen, *Doris Humphrey: An Artist First* (Middletown, Connecticut: Wesleyan University Press, 1972), p. 255.
46. *Isadora*, pp. 75-77.
47. *Martha Graham*, p. 96.
48. *The Diary*, IV, p. 222.

49.   "Pearl Primus," *American Dancers* (New York, 1946), p. 15.

50.   James Haskins, *Katherine Dunham* (New York: Harcourt, Brace, Jovanovich, 1982), p. 27.

51.   *The Diary*, IV, p. 154.

52.   *American Dancer* (March, 1938), p. 46.

53.   "Pearl Primus," *Dance Magazine* (April, 1946), p. 31.

54.   *The Portable Jung* (New York: Viking, 1972), p. 276.

55.   *The Portable Jung*, p. 285.

56.   *The Diary*, V, p. 192.

57.   *Modern Dance Terminology*, p. 49.

58.   *Modern Dance Terminology* p. 59.

59.   *The Diary*, III, p. 235.

60.   *American Dancer* (March, 1958), p. 43.

61.   *Katherine Dunham*, p. 151.

62.   *Dance and Dancer* (May, 1950), p. 19.

63.   *American Dancer* (March, 1938), p. 46.

64.   *Cities of the Interior*, p. 175

A Map of Music — Strange Dimensions of
Politics and War
by Wayne McEvilly

No one **has** written more movingly, more sincerely, more translucently, of music than Anais. To those of us who in the 60s turned in desperation to the East she kept alive the faith that it is in music we have our source of supply and renewal, that music stands supreme itself, ancillary to nothing else. Of music —

"THERE IS NO OTHER WAY TO REACH THE INFINITE."

***

Music became the standard by which all else was measured, and only love itself reflected and balanced it out in human experience. Thus Anais had throughout her life this transcendent, supreme, and living standard to guide her through the maze. Wherever her gaze fell and her attention lingered, that place, event, or personality stood out by virtue of her own enlightening field of perception. Fortunate the phenomena which fall within the province of such a perspect.

***

Lord, in your eyes I must be one of many. Of many? Are they
given the consciousness of their own perishing? Perishing? They too
perish? This remote object? This mute thing? This rock striated with
the effects of unknown drama to which the earth must have been sub-
ject before the coming of consciousness? It will outlive us, will outlive
all the living, will sit in mute repose when all that could have recorded
its being here shall have vanished, and there be not so much as one
lonely snail creeping across the page of its charted or uncharted destiny
leaving its trace of translucence, its silvery trail of slime.
("The Chinese in Montana")

***

Today is August 6, 1983.   Thirty-eight years ago The United States
of America, by command of Harry S. Truman, dropped a bomb on
Hiroshima, and then another on Nagasaki.   The American collective
psyche has not computed this fact as yet.   "The Chinese in Montana"
meant to begin to take it into account.   In one of the notebooks kept
anonymously by a traveling scribe we find:

LOS ALAMOS: *The Atomic City*
Birthplace of the
Atomic Age.

***

Mr. Truman said —
"The maneuvers in a battle are like the maneuvers in politics.   In the
military they have what they call a five paragraph order.
In the first paragraph you make an estimate of the enemy, his condition
and what he can do.
In the second paragraph you make an estimate of your own condition
and what you can do.
In the third paragraph you decide what you are going to do.
The fourth paragraph — you set up your logistics and supply sources
to carry out what you are going to do.
And in the fifth paragraph you tell where you are going to be so that
everybody can reach you.
That is all there is to politics."

A DEFINITION OF POLITICS WITH REFERENCE
TO ITS MODES AND MEANS BY HARRY S. TRUMAN

***

Anais delighted in communicating intelligence.   Her subject range
was enormous.   The final volume of her *Diary* alone suggests for future

journalists, novelists, these subjects and more — Antidotes to loneliness and lack of confidence, love itself, and music, the family, the refusal to despair, specifics like Schubert, the Grateful Dead, Gore Vidal, Richard Nixon, Norman Mailer, Truman Capote, India, Catholicism, Zen, L.S.D., East & West, China, Japan, Mexico, travel, the metaphysics of voyaging, correspondence, Montana.

Whatever her subject, it is taken up in a transcendent and transcending atmosphere of faith and consciousness, love and attention, devotion and concern, awareness and discernment, lucidity and affection, clarity, wit, and brilliance. It is stellar.

***

She demonstrated destiny. I will never forget the day in Bozeman, Montana, that I received a letter from her in which she wrote of my destiny as a writer, my destiny as a musician. I was stunned. It's a fact that without that letter and its content, essentially repeated in a torrent of letters and purple postcards (they became purple snow-flakes in a real snow country), I would never have considered I had any destiny at all. Something more than magic happened in that moment. But then, as the letters continued, I found that Anais demonstrated destiny to all of us. It is a good word to keep foremost in mind. Those who are reading this will probably remember the account Anais gives of her times with other writers in Paris:

June 12 1970

Dear Wayne: The first letter I have written in 2 weeks! I was in London for 4 days of publicity. In Paris for 10 days. No sooner awake than a journalist was waiting downstairs — Long interviews on tape. Then a rush to the radio station, then 2 *full* days of television, walking the streets of Paris, visiting old haunts — sitting in a cafe. Beautiful weather — a cocktail of critics — an evening with my translator. The side of a writer's life I like the least but in this case transfigured by my real joy at recovering my links with France.

***

In 1972 I was in Ukiah California to conduct a workshop in writing which Anais had arranged. We had discussed the carrying out of this mission in playful terms, speaking of Chinese scribes in a fictive army devoted to transcendent values, how they would take their notes and silently pass on to another scene. The challenge of arranging material recalcitrant to language and communicating concerning it was indeed a keen one. We were to speak of concerns so finely subtle as to require for their very existence the greenhouse environment of absolute solitude. I tried for a while to joust my way out of it by means of grotesque efforts to see it all under the aesthetic category of the comedic. It seemed natural to take Laurence Sterne at his word as our point of departure —

—for never do I hit upon any invention or device which tendeth to the furtherance of good writing, but I instantly make it public; willing that all mankind should write as well as myself. —Which they certainly will, when they think as little.

So we went into town and this is what happened —

Ukiah. Palace Hotel. Lobby. Ringing of the switchboard, perhaps for the politician whose name is on the vase of orange balloons on sticks. Two scribes in vinyl chairs taking notes. Across the lobby the only other occupant, her back to the window, casts a single suspicious glance in the direction of our activity. We note the fact.

Synchronicity. A sign informs us that On The Lane we might find The Black Bart Room, The Mendocino Room, The Timber Room, The Palace Beauty Shop. By the door was a rack of free tracts. I picked some of them up, and this is what I found — The Holy Ghost And Fire, Plan Of Salvation, Good News For The Sick, and Evidence For The Holy Ghost, all approved by The Committee On Doctrine. As I did not find this material particularly edifying, I looked up to see a white haired woman crossing the lobby. I heard and old man clear his throat.

"Cancel that call!" said a man in brown slacks noisily descending the stairs. He disappeared, it seemed, leaving no emptiness.

These effusions went on, and on, and on, for this was a weekend workshop. A message arrived from Anais. *"Don't deny the poetics. Those who turn it down are mistaken. The poet is the only visionary."*

The chemistry of that weekend was transcendent. These were concretions, vital electricities which intimately cling to the artist form and survive the ravages of time. It is the energy of a magic circle. It was not a gathering of intellectuals invoking Hesse, but a circle of players with beads at the ready. No conclusions were drawn, yet there was this sense that perhaps this had been the first movement in a symphonic return to childhood. That the yearning in one soul could correspond to the yearning in another soul. Discoveries. There were these cricket musicians singing in the night, these symphonists so close to God. As we wrote we discerned that we were on a space ship following the sound current. The work agreement was to write twenty-one pages in one day, twenty-one the following day, and the third day, having gathered such a decent amount of evidence, to powwow. We heard many stories, we walked through many gardens. Stories of Pony, Montana. Of Chinamen buried alive in Butte. One was hurled into the falls — Great Falls, Montana. Anais also wrote of the "Gypsy Tent in Space" as the place where music might find its oasis.

In the same year India refused visas to American scholars. I was denied entry for a while, but by dint of persistence and through a strong proposal to pursue the values of music in ancient Sanskrit texts I was able to spend a year in Bharata, Mother India. I still treasure a purple postcard on which Anais has written that she is praying for my visa to India. At the same time, the light of her lucid intelligence insisted on an utterly individuated voyage of self-discovery that entailed no abrogation to a ready made system designed to clone types. Anais never settled for the type, not even the archetype. True, the type and archetype have been what we have gotten used to in fiction, but Anais broke that mold. Not the type, but the individual is portrayed — she attends to those subtle individuating elements which make us who we are much more so than do any typical characteristics we may exhibit. What Anais holds forth is truly revolutionary — it begins in the contemplation of the fact that music and love have political power. This is not going to be easy. War and hatred are not easy. Neither is the struggle to let love live in a world without war. "Transcendent" is not "abstract." Merely dreaming musicians will never change the world. Only playing, singing musicians will change the world.

***

She perceived and articulated a union of poets, artists, musicians, in an ever-widening circle. She showed a growing number an essential oneness, a vivid spiritual union. Dealing always in realities, and dreaming that what had been the dream would turn out to be real, she had witnessed many miracles along the way. Here is a letter dated November 6, 1970—

> All these beautiful letters from you, like smoke issuing from the fires of the book itself. No, your letters do not cheat the Diary because it is the same world. A continuity. At one moment you speak of that moment reached in Fez; it happens only when the external life matches or harmonizes with the inner one. Fez did. It matched the dreams so I was able to unite them. That is why it is so important to create the outer life to match one's inner longings, so that they reach a marriage. Diary is being given at College of Psychologists as map route to inner journey. But even if that is true, pepole forget how much I struggled to make the outer world conform to my dreams or images, discarding what did not belong and whoever did not belong, in order to create a harmonious world. It is not an end to introspection I thought, it was the bridge between inner and outer. This I have trouble conveying to students recently at Philadelphia. They can only see Either Or, and erect bar-

riers. It is when the circulation is established that miracles happen. Love, Anais."

***

Chapter 52
The Chinese in Montana

"THE GRIEF OF THE VICTIMS OF THE BOMB."
Scene — TAMAI TOWERS, DENVER
Softly, swiftly, a young Japanese man enters a room where an old man lies in bed, his hands in repose, with closed eyes.
The young man's voice —
"THREE DAYS AGO THEY BOMBED NAGASAKI."
Only the stones could say what the silence held that enveloped them now.
The old man's voice —
"WHO BOMBED NAGASAKI?"

***

Who could speak of the grief of the victims of the bomb? Who knew? What human tongue could utter an anguish echoing beyond the corridors of time? The stones would have to speak. There was no other way but to hear the stories the bricks would tell, the tales of trees, echoing vibrations real as wind.
For the grief of the victims of the bomb had been the grief of all humanity.

***

East and West

In public life Anais Nin was pacific and acquiescent, and, for the most part, reserved in her expression. This silence did not connote assent. On one purple postcard she has written —

"I HAVE NEVER FOUND IT WORTHWHILE TO ARGUE WITH THE ENEMY."

Anais warned us of the dangers of the butterfly psyche's flirtations with the Orient. She never did suggest, however, that we throw the baby out with the bath water. The enemy she faced was not the yoga, the zen, the tapasya itself. No. She incorporated all of that into her daily discipline. The enemy was the spirit of fascist bondage, of all that assigned a ready-made path and ordered others to trod it to the letter of a law of devious invention. The portrayals in the Diary are brief and to the point. Words are not wasted. The assessments ring just and true. She leaves no doubt what she thinks of Nixon, Vidal, Mailer but she wastes neither time nor words on them.

Anais created love. She clarified music. She clarified politics. Looking at America through her transcending lens she saw — not envisioned, saw — a new America already in existence. Not yet in power, but in full plenitude of being. And she knew well before the students emblazoned it in paint at the foot of the Berkeley campus clock tower that we must

STOP NIXON

IT'S UP

TO US

"It's up to us" means it's up to me, to you. Only I can give to the universe the one meaningful gift — a fulfilled person, myself. Whether it is stopping aggression or performing all the Beethoven Sonatas, the processes remain the same — the beginnings of action in a faith rooted in the capacity of the individual to create worlds not yet dreamed. So the plenitude of our existence is not sufficient. Necessary, but not sufficient. We must proceed from the dream outward. Simple as it sounds, to act is to have the power.

***

Anais transcended the image of teacher. Her role while she was on this planet had more to do with a vivid blazing of trails linking a variety of disciplines. She integrated circuits, creating new lines of communication. She put people in touch with themselves, and then with each other. She did not theorize or philosophize about unity in the arts; she was a unifying force clarifying strange dimensions of politics and war, and showed how music and love alone could change the world. She revealed dimensions of the art of music to those of us who inhabit it. The cartographer of the heart, of the emotions, of the subtlest plays of human light and shade, was best equipped to draw the map of music.

***

Words have the power to realize themselves in realities. They are energy releasers and power directors. Just a word in a letter — "DESTINY" — can change a life. Just a word on a wall — "TRANS—CENDENCE" — can open vast horizons to the butterfly psyche. Sometimes an entire sentence would have the force of a mantra. I remember one purple postcard here —

"DUST! HOW WONDERFUL THIS THEME! ENDLESS!"

That was a revelation that served not only literary ends, but opened the inner eye to the outer world. How could you thank a friend who revealed to you glories in the dust?

Anais Nin and Film: Open Questions
by Robert A. Haller

Anais Nin's interest in film as an arena of artistic expression is something we can track through her life. In the 20s she closely followed French surrealist cinema; in the 40s she appeared in Maya Deren's *Ritual in Transfigured Time*; in the 50s she performed again — in Kenneth Anger's *Inauguration of the Pleasure Dome* and in a series of films by Ian Hugo, including *Bells of Atlantis*; in the 60s she appeared in more of Hugo's films, and wrote appreciatively about filmmakers Henry Jaglom, Ingmar Bergman, and Jean Genet.

In her writings, Nin articulated repeatedly her admiration of filmmakers who used cinema to create realms of the imagination, to work with the imagery of dreams, to enter into the minds of characters. It is, however, very striking that there are some *very* important endeavors in film that she did not write about in her published diary and essays.

What I have in mind is the effulgent flowering of independent, avant garde film in the 60s. Nin lived in the midst of the movement. Ian Hugo — her husband — made such films (about whom she did write, though never acknowledging her marriage to him); Hugo was also a leader of this community of film-makers (which she did not write about). This is notably striking because independent film-making was so similar to Nin's own experience in the 40s when she was engaged in typesetting, printing, and publishing her own books. A similar aesthetic is at the roots of indepdendent cinema. It is an alternative to commercial/industrial film-making, an alternative in which the film-maker himself performs all or most of the steps involved in making the film — saving money and retaining full control.

In the 60s this kind of film was significantly influenced by the concept of the film as, not drama, but rather as a direct expression of the film-maker's poetic vision. Of all this work there is no mention in Nin's writing.[1]

At the end of the 60s a new kind of film-making emerged — a kind closely related to the earlier direct vision. This new form was that of the diary film. Necessarily, the diary film must be photographed at once, *during* the events depicted. In this it is very different from a written diary which is always composed *after* the events described. In a diary film one can add, later, a voice narration that will provide some of the retrospection of a written text. Film diaries, nevertheless, offer a particularly immediate sense of experience; different but related to written diaries, film diaries provoke an enlarged sense of what the diary form can and can not be.

Again, of this kind of film Nin apparently wrote nothing. How much of it she saw we do not know, but she did know the films existed, and she personally knew at least one of the form's most acclaimed practitioners — Jonas Mekas.

Why Nin declined to comment on this body of work is an open question. There are some possible answers, but I do not feel these hypotheses add up to a complete explanation. The complete diaries may add to our understanding of this matter, but I doubt if her public silence on some of these films will ever be understood. Films like Mekas' *Diaries, Notes and Sketches* (1968) and Andrew Noren's *Kodak Ghost Poems,* later titled *Huge Pupils* (1967-1968) are watershed films which have marked turning points in independent cinema.

While this kind of film grew and flowered during the last decade of Nin's life, at a time when she was struggling against the effects of cancer, the works were accessible to her (and she may have talked about these films in one of her journal-writing workshops in the early 70s). Why did she not write about them?

My hypotheses about her silence are two. First, there is the matter of Nin's painful, difficult, fifteen year estrangement from Maya Deren. In 1945-1946 Deren filmed Nin for her film *Ritual in Transfigured Time* (see volume IV of the *Diary*). Nin's performance in the film in no way referred to her real life. Her role was limited to that of a supporting part, a stern, somewhat aloof older woman, a mystery figure dressed in black. She and the other performers in the film found their appearance objectionable. "There was an ugliness in the vision, in the camera eye. . . ." (IV, 156).

Deren and Nin were never reconciled. Mutual friends tried to persuade them to restore their friendship, but all failed. Val Telberg, the film-maker-photographer who illustrated the 1958 edition of *House of Incest*, believes pride on both sides was the obstacle.[2]

Up to 1961, the time of her death, Deren was the single most active and articulate spokesperson for independent/avant garde film. Avoiding contact with Deren inevitably meant avoiding much contact with the independent film-making, community. It also led to a posture in which Nin grew to distrust the values of film-makers. In March, 1946, she wrote in her diary, of the early stages of the filming of *Ritual in Transfigured Time,* that the shooting was unorganized, chaotic, empty, and there was no dramatic exchange. "I wanted to tell Maya: Use my words to describe what is happening! But of course film-makers have a contempt for words" (IV, 135-136). Words, of course, were Nin's chosen instrument of expression.

My second hypothesis relates to words and film. Nin's chosen instrument of expression was the pen, not the camera, and while she acknowledged the achievements of cinema, she tended to feel these were chiefly due to the contributions of screenwriters, not directors. For instance, in her book *In Favor of the Sensitive Man,* she collects writings on three film directors, who are all writers as well: Ingmar Bergman, Jean Genet, and Henry Jaglom. In Volum VI of the *Diary* she discusses Michelangelo Antonioni's *La Notte.* In the opening sentence she isolates the function of writing: "In this film the artistry of the director suffers from being allied to a writer without distinction, to Antonioni the screenwriter." (VI, 283).

In "Poetics of the Film," a lecture given at the University of Chicago and printed in *Film Culture,* No 31, 1963-1964, Nin discusses Ian Hugo's films, and then turns to six other films and film-makers. Of Jules Dassin's *Phaedra* she approves of a love scene photographed through a fire. Of Hilary Harris she cites his discovery of rhythms and form in the patterns of moving highways. Thereafter her attention turns to writers: to Beatriz Guido's script for *End of Innocence,* to Marguerite Duras' script of *Hiroshima Mon Amour,* to Alain Robbe-Grillet's script for *Last Year at Marienbad,* and to Mary Ellen Bute for working on a film of *Finnegan's Wake* (emphasis on the book, not the film or film-maker). While three of these four writers were women,

the point is more literary than feminist. This is reiterated three para-
graphs from the end of the paper: "Hugo emphasizes simultaneity
of experience as Joyce did in literature."

Independent, avant garde film, where writing was consistently
subordinated to imagery (a kind of film which often was silent, wordless), thus was a kind of expression Nin was predisposed to sidestep.
From her personal experience, as well as her preference for the work
of writers, she tended to avoid, with certain exceptions, this medium
otherwise so similar to her own. This is frustrating because when
she did write about Kenneth Anger, or Ian Hugo, her discussions were
evocative and insightful. Nin could see beneath the surface of the photographed image. In 1962, writing about Jean Gabriel Albicocco's
The Girl With the Golden Eyes, Nin said it was

> a film that proves that realism is not reality. . . . Only the
> poet and the artist know how to illumine a realistic scene
> . . . so that it suggests that other dimensions . . . in all this the
> inner dimensions, inner fantasies, play as strong a role as the
> outer images.[3]

To Nin these inner dimensions and inner fantasies were often only
visible in the context of a literary framework.

NOTES

1.   Some of the film-makers overlooked are Marie Menken, Gunvor
Nelson, Warren Sonbert, Ken Jacobs, Bruce Baillie, Stan Brakhage, Taylor Mead,
Carolee Schneemann.

2.   "Val Telberg: Two Interviews and Photographs," *Field of Vision,*
No. 7 (Summer, 1979), p. 9.

3.   *Scenario* (March-April, 1962), 3, 2: 3.

Anais Nin's House of Incest and
Ingmar Bergman's Persona:
Two Variations on a Theme
by Nancy Scholar

So now we are inextricably woven...
I AM THE OTHER FACE OF YOU
Our faces are soldered together by soft hair,
  soldered together,
showing two profiles of the same soul.[1]

There is an intriguing congruence between this poetic description of
merged identities in Anais Nin's prose-poem *House of Incest* (1936)
and an identical visual image in Ingmar Bergman's film *Persona*
(1966).[2] The similarity extends beyond an overlap of image. There
are many commonalities between these disparate artists and works
— as well as interesting differences — which are illuminated by this
imagistic convergence. Both film and book present a "distillation"
of the themes which haunted the artists in many other works. "It is
the seed of all my work, the poem from which the novels were born,"[3]
Nin has said about her first work of fiction. Bergman has also described *Persona* in poetic terms,[4] but this masterpiece came after
more than twenty years of prolific filmmaking, and hence, has an artistic maturity which is lacking in Nin's first effort. Yet there is an
intuitive, visionary quality to *House of Incest* which gives it an extraordinary luminosity.

Bergman has referred to *Persona*, along with *Through a Glass Darkly*,
Winter Light, and *The Silence*, as a "chamber work." This description
applies to *House of Incest* as well: "They are chamber music — music
in which, with an extremely limited number of voices and figures, one
explores the essence of a number of motifs. The backgrounds are ex-
trapolated, put into a sort of fog. The rest is distillation."[5] Nin describes *House* as containing the "purest essence" of her meaning, the
"distillation of her experience."[6] In this "EDIFICE WITHOUT DI-

MENSION," she focuses on a small number of figures and puts the
background into a "fog." The same could be said for later works,
including *Winter of Artifice* and the five-volume *Cities of the Interior*, but *House of Incest* is the most condensed and poetic.

It is also the most unconventional of Nin's books, and the least
amenable to analysis and definition. The same is true for *Persona*,
which marks a radical departure for Bergman from more traditional
forms and subject matter. Both works may have discouraged critical
approach, because they tend to resist analysis and definition, as part
of their meaning. Nin and Berman alike wish to explore a realm of
experience below or beyond rationality; they attempt to break down
and through the comfortable masks and surfaces by which most of
us live. For such purposes, they both require forms which depart
from the norm. Exprimental themes and forms are frightening to
some, unsatisfactory to others. In addition, both film and book share
a reputation for difficulty which has added to the confusion. Oliver
Evans calls *House* the "most difficult of Miss Nin's books."[7] and John
Simon refers to *Persona* as "probably the most difficult film ever
made."[8] It is hardly surprising, after such ominous warnings, that
these works have not received as much recogntion as they deserve.

II

The appearance of formlessness in the prose-poem is, to some extent, deceptive; each of the seven sections which compose the book
has the underlying coherence of the dream. But the meaning of these
"visionary symbolic dream sequences"[9] must be "unravelled" by
the reader. Nin created *House* out of a record of her dreams which she
kept for a year, so it is her unconscious — transformed, to be sure —
which provides the deepest structure in this work. Jung's words were
her inspiration: "To proceed from the dream outward."[10] But Nin
herself doubted whether her dream exploration actually moved outward: "In *House of Incest* I describe what it is to be trapped in the
dream, unable to relate it to life, unable to reach 'daylight.'"[11] Even
though she may not have reached "daylight" in *House*, Nin was able
to explore and suggest the rich potentiality of the dream terrain, which
she continued to excavate in later writing.

Although there is no indication that Bergman created *Persona* out of personal dreams, he certainly seems to have been in a nightmarish state during its inception. He was confined to the hospital for two months with a disease of the inner ear which produced dizziness and a sensation of imbalance. "I was lying there," he says, "half dead, and suddenly I started to think of two faces, two intermingled faces, and that was the beginning, the place where it started."[12] Most of *Persona* takes place in that twilight zone between wakefulness and the dream state, life and death. It is difficult to separate dream and reality in the film, and this is another aspect of its reputed difficulty. Bergman has commented: "The reality we experience today is in fact as absurd, as horrible, and as obtrusive as our dreams . . . And one is strongly aware . . . that there are no boundaries between dream and reality today."[13]

But how much more difficult to recreate the wordless dream through language than through the visual image. Hence the use of photomontages in *House* to assist in this near-impossible task, and the reliance on hypnotic, incantatory language in the first sequence to facilitate reconstruction of a dream state. The barrage of images which flash rapidly on the screen during the first moments of *Persona* serve a similar function. They are both an effort to jolt the audience out of comfortable, ordinary existence and into a condition receptive to the unconscious, at the same time as they are a reflection of the artist's own unconscious creative process. In other words, for Nin and Bergman alike, the unconscious is their own starting point, their subject matter, and their focus in the audience at once. As Bergman comments, "You sit in a dark room and you have this little bright, bright square before you . . . And of course, it goes right inside you and right down in your emotional mind — in your unconscious."[14] Nin is more explicit about the audience involvement in this process in a discussion of Bergman's films:

> It is the emotional, not the analytical, journey which brings deliverance from secret corrosions. Bergman's films have that intent; we should accept the fact of a profound emotional journey into mostly unexplored realms, into all we

have not dared to feel, to say, to act, to embrace in life.
It is a journey through dark regions.   But it should stir
in us all the unknown elements in ourselves . . . this is the
world which Jung has called our shadow.   Bergman presents
the shadow of the selves we do not wish to acknowledge.[15]

III

House as well as *Persona* has the intent which Nin describes here.
Jung's concept of shadow and persona are directly relevant to both
works, and profoundly significant as a whole for Bergman and Nin.
Bergman was reading Jung during the time he was working on the
film, and has acknowledged the Jungian basis for its title.[16]   "Persona" originally meant actor's mask, which Jung extended to the
personality we construct to meet the world, "designed on the one
hand to make a definite impression upon others, and, on the other
hand, to conceal the true nature of the individual."[17]   Nin summarizes
the effects of developing this social mask in the fourth published
diary:

> The acceptance of this social role delivers us to the demands
> of the collective, and makes us a stranger to our own reality.
> The consequent split in the personality may find the ego in
> agreement with general community expectations, while the
> repressed shadow turns dissenter.
> Failure to acknowledge this dark alter ego creates the ten-
> dency to project it onto someone in the immediate en-
> vironment, the mirror opposite to one's self.[18]

It is this split between the socially acceptable facade and the hidden
shadow self projected outwards which is dramatized in both *House*
and *Persona*.   Persona, shadow, and double are prominent themes
in the work of both Nin and Bergman, but in *House* and *Persona*
they are more fully explored.   The two women in each work can
be seen as personifications of mask and shadow respectively, at the
same time as they play out the drama of identification and projection

between two selves. They are each dramas of division and isolation, both internal and external. Fusion within the self, resolution of the feelings of division, and unity between two selves, prove impossible to sustain, but it is this quest for wholeness which underlies both film and book.

From one perspective, Alma, the nurse in *Persona,* and the narrator in *House* represent the external, daily personality or persona. Elizabeth, the actress in the film, and Sabina in the prose-poem personify the shadow figure. We first catch a glimpse of Elizabeth literally masked in theatrical make-up and playing the role of Electra. But in suddenly ceasing to speak or act, she seems to resign the artificiality of her customary pose. Yet she remains protected and concealed behind the silence she maintains almost undisturbed in the course of the film. The psychiatrist in the hospital where she is staying at the beginning of the film interprets her condition as the abyss between "what you are for others and what you are for yourself . . . the continual burning need to be unmasked. At last to be seen through, reduced, perhaps extinguished. Every tone of voice a lie, an act of treason. Every gesture false." But she warns her: "Your hiding place isn't watertight enough. Life starts leaking in everywhere. And you're forced to react. No one asks whether it's genuine or not, whether you're true or false." She suggests that Elizabeth's silence is but another role which she will play out until it loses interest for her.

Some of the fears which the psychiatrist points to in her analysis of Elizabeth are expressed by the characters in *House.* Jeanne, who embodies the shadow side of the narrator's personality in the fourth section of *House,* is a verbal counterpart to Elizabeth: "I have such a fear of finding another like myself, and such a desire to find one! I am so utterly lonely, but I also have such a fear that my isolation be broken through, and I no longer be the head and ruler of my universe. I am in great terror of your understanding by which you penetrate into my world; and then I stand revealed and I have to share my kingdom with you" (HI, 46-47). The desire to be known and fear of being known, the yearning for the protection of the mask, and the relief of stripping the mask: these universal dualities produce some of the tension and struggle in both works.

Persona and *House* reflect the ambivalent attitude of Nin and Bergman alike towards being understood: there is a purposeful obfuscation
of meaning, at the same time as there is a revelation of deepest meaning. Both seem suspicious of the craving to scrutinize and penetrate
which is characteristic of artist and critic. The writer in *Through a
Glass Darkly* is shown to be guilty of this, as is Elizabeth in the film.
Nin rails against this tendency in critics throughout her writing, including this passage in which she dissusses the critics' reaction to
Bergman: "The critics are annoyed by mystery. If significance eludes
them they feel powerless . . . The one who seeks analytical clarity
remains only a tourist, a spectator."[19] In place of critical detachment,
Bergman and Nin alike demand immersion in the experience on the
part of reader and audience.

The second section of *House*, which is the primary focus of this
discussion, revolves around the narrator, who is a writer, and Sabina,
a masked personage, who is her shadow self. The narrator, like Alma
the nurse in *Persona,* is protected by the semblance of normality
and wholeness which she presents at the start of the narrative: "Step
out of your role and rest yourself on the core of your true desires
. . . I will take them up" (HI. 27). Sabina is the more obviously disguised: "Sabina's face was suspended in the darkness of the garden
. . . The luminous mask of her face, waxy, immobile, with eyes like
sentinels" (HI, 13, 22). They are both masked figures, but the narrator's mask is her artistic persona, which enables her to play the role
of integrator and nurturer, while Sabina's mask is her primeval sensuality. She embodies the shadow side of "proper" femininity. Nin
describes her as sexually overpowering: "Every gesture she made
quickened the rhythm of the blood and aroused a beat chant like
the beat of the heart of the desert, a chant which was the sound of
her feet treading down into the blood the imprint of her face" (HI,
18, 21). There is also an aspect of cruelty and power hunger in her:
"Her necklace thrown around the world's neck, unmeltable. She
carried it like a trophy wrung of groaning machinery, to match the
inhuman rhythm of her march" (HI, 22).

Both Sabina and Elizabeth have an inhuman quality, related to
their silence and waxy immobility. They represent the dreamed self,

woman as OTHER. The mysterious, unformed aspects of both provide invitations for audience projection and fantasy. The narrator in *House* and Alma in *Persona* project onto this flexible image buried facets of themselves, both positive and negative. Alma identifies with the fantasy self she sees in the beautiful, successful actress, Elizabeth, and boasts that she could change herself into her if she tried hard. The narrator in *House* expresses her identification with the other in beautiful poetic language:

> Your beauty drowns me, drowns the core of me. When your beauty burns me I dissolve as I never dissolved before man. From all men I was different and myself, but I see in you that part of me which is you. I feel you in me; I feel my own voice becoming heavier, as if I were drinking you in, every delicate thread of resemblance being soldered by fire and one no longer detects the fissure (HI, 25-26).

The writer in *House* yearns to merge with her mirror-opposite, the physical embodiment of her dreamed self. Mirror love is a persistent theme in Nin's writing, which gains clarity over the years. In *Seduction of the Minotaur*, the last novel of *Cities of the Interior*, she summarizes the meaning of this attraction to Sabina:

> It was a desire for an impossible union: she wanted to lose herself in Sabina and BECOME Sabina. This wanting to BE Sabina she had mistaken for love of Sabina's night beauty. She wanted to lie beside her and become her and be one with her and both arise as ONE woman; she wanted to add herself to Sabina, re-enforce the woman in herself, the submerged woman, intensify this woman Lillian she could not liberate fully . . . She had loved in Sabina an unborn Lillian. By adding herself to Sabina she would become a more potent woman.[20]

The narrator's longing, from this perspective, is not so much for another person, as for the liberation of the buried parts of herself.

This is one of the patterns which binds the dream fragments of *House* together, and for that matter, much of Nin's writing: woman's struggle to liberate the submerged aspects of herself, to resurrect and confront qualities considered socially unacceptable, such as overt sexuality and creative ambition.   The dramas of twinship in this volume, and elsewhere in Nin, are variants on the theme of this drive towards self-fulfillment; but mirror love turns out not to be a satisfactory method of attaining that completion of self, since it leads to isolation, guilt, and self-division.   Sabina is but a facet of the narrator's self-reflected image, and she is left confined in the coils of self-love: "Worlds self-made and self-nourished are so full of ghosts and monsters," she tells Jeanne (HI, 47).   The writer in the last section of *House* cries out: "If only we could all escape from this house of incest, where we only love ourselves in the òther" (HI, 70).

As unsatisfactory as this narcissistic form of love is shown to be in *House*, it may perhaps be a necessary stage of development, particularly for the artist who, almost by definition, must be self-reflective, self-absorbed, especially at the beginning of the creative process. From this vantage point, *House of Incest* is about the birth of an artist, just as it is about the birth of the artist's first work.   In uniting with Sabina, the narrator hopes to attain the visibility as woman and artist that she lacked: "Sabina, you made your impression upon the world.   I passed through it like a ghost . . . DOES ANYONE KNOW WHO I AM?" (HI, 26).   Similarly, if Alma in the film is regarded as a projection of Elizabeth, the actress/artist, then the film, too, may be about her creative birth.   Nin describes *Persona* interestingly enough, as just that: "Part of the mystery is that he takes us into the act of birth, birth of a film as well as of a character."[21]   Elizabeth's alienation from her roles as actress, wife, and mother also makes sense in terms of her conflicts as woman and artist, just as the narrator's struggles in *House* may be seen as a duel between the demands of the woman and artist within herself.

Although the same narcissistic impulse informs the film as the book, whether from Alma's or Elizabeth's perspective, it differs from *House* in that the dynamic between two women seems much more apparent, perhaps due to the greater tangibility of the figures in the visual medium. Alma's identification and projection onto Elizabeth is concretely displayed when she begins to dress and behave like her, until finally their images on the screen become inextricable. It is this loss of definition between the two selves which is at once feared and desired, as is the case in the book. Nin has commented about *House* and *Persona*: "In *House of Incest* I treated the theme of exchange of personalities, as Bergman did later in the film *Persona*. Sabina and the writer of the poem are in constant danger of identifying with each other and *becoming the other.*"[22] Total identification in both cases leads to confusion and loss of identity, a sensation of drowning in the other. Alma's captivation by her mirror-opposite forces her into a confrontation with her own shadow self, and a loss of the comforts of her mask.

Gradually the protective coating of her nurse's uniform wears off, and she is revealed both to herself and to the audience. Elizabeth's silence forces her in upon herself, and this is the source of her terror and her desperation. She begins to reveal things about her past which she had long ago forgotten. She recounts an early sexual experience and a subsequnet abortion. The next day, she discovers a letter from Elizabeth to her psychiatrist in which her psyche is discussed in abstract, analytic terms. She feels vulnerable and betrayed, and takes brutal revenge. Alma places a piece of broken glass in Elizabeth's path as retribution, and in that act the persona of the nurse is stripped bare. Bergman conveys this crack in her mask visually by having the image of her face through the window crack and burn immediately after this event. It is a powerful visual metaphor, suggesting the collapse of personality, reality, and art simultaneously.

After the film burns, there is a duplication of some of the same disturbing images Bergman used in the opening sequence of the film. Once again the audience is made aware that they are watching a film, at the same time as they are presented with an image which burns right through the surface of art, reality, and mask. When the camera refocuses, in place of Alma's face in the window, Elizabeth appears. The audience is unsettled; it is impossible to sort out exactly what is "real." There is an increasing confusion between the identities of Alma and Elizabeth, between imagined and actual events. Yet to attempt to untangle what is dream and what actually "happens" in the film is to miss the point. Boundaries have been eradicated in both these works between real and dreamed events, between mask and shadow, and between the two women.

IV

The center of the drama in both film and book, and the point of convergence between visual and verbal image, comes at the moment of total identification between the two women. The fusion of the narrator and Sabina is described in words which provide a perfect counterpart to the screen variation on this theme: "So now we are inextricably woven . . . Our faces are soldered together by soft hair, soldered together, showing two profiles of the same soul" (HI, 28). In the film, the faces of the two women are literally merged in a single face, at first obviously off-kilter, then disturbingly integrated. It is an indelible image of integration and self-division at once, a picture of unity between mask and shadow, between Alma and Elizabeth, and of fragmentation and loss of self. There is a haunting terror and beauty in this image which is unmatched by any other shot in Bergman's impressive repertoire.

This visual fusion of identities comes after one of the most excruciating scenes in the film. Alma's identification with Elizabeth is at this point nearly total. She is dressed exactly like her, and appears to have absorbed her inner self as well. She discovers Elizabeth looking at the picture of her son which she had torn apart at the start of the film. Alma uncovers the picture which Elizabeth attempts to hide, and proceeds to tell Elizabeth how she felt before, during, and after her pregnancy. We watch Elizabeth's pained reaction as Alma reminds her of the social pressures that led Elizabeth to get pregnant to begin with (the accusation that she was not a complete woman, even though she was a successful artist), the hostile feelings she had towards the unborn child within her, and the disgust and hate she felt for the newborn infant. There is probably no deeper shadow Alma could reveal in Elizabeth: her lack of the "appropriate" motherly feelings. Bergman replays the exact same scene, only this time the camera focuses on Alma's face instead of Elizabeth's. The audience wonders how she could know these things about Elizabeth. Is she projecting her own deepest feelings? It is impossible to say, but the revelation of her own abortion suggests her involvement in the accusation. The two women are one in the overlap of their hidden selves. At the end of this scene, the two faces merge; they are inextricably woven.

The emotional intensity of this scene is accentuated by the intimacy of the camera shots. The faces of the two women fill the screen, and we are enveloped in their images. In this way, we are brought into the process taking place between them. If the film's full effectiveness is to be experienced, the audience must identify and project into the characters, just as they do with each other. The same invitation for audience participation takes place in *House*. At the high point in the merging of identities, the following words appear centered on the page:

I AM THE OTHER FACE OF YOU. . .
THIS IS THE BOOK YOU WROTE
AND YOU ARE THE WOMAN
I AM

(HI, 28)

The interchange of identities between Sabina and the narrator is extended through this method to include the reader as well. We are encouraged to discover and lose ourselves at once in the narrator's words. Complete identification with the narrator may lead to a discovery of the hidden artist within us, or to a sense of unity and mergence with our shadow self. The meaning of this peak moment in both book and film is the product of a coalescence of artist, audience, and actors.

But the center does not hold. The moment disintegrates, perhaps because of the difficulty of maintaining a feeling of wholeness in a shattered world, or within a fragmented self. The dissolution of the bond also suggests the fear of intimacy, a powerful *leitmotif* in the work of both Nin and Bergman. At least as strong as this fear of closeness is the fear of homosexuality, which appears as an under-current in *Persona* and *House*. The erotic component in *Persona* is implied by visual innuendo, such as the night scene in which the two women embrace and their figures overlap in a dreamlike manner. The eroticism in the prose-poem is quite blatant: "Around my pulse she put a flat steel bracelet and my pulse beat . . . thumping like a savage in orgiastic frenzy" (HI, 23). The sexual suggestiveness in both *House* and *Persona* is shrouded with ambiguity, partly because of the dream atmosphere which pervades book and film. Whether the women touch in either case is irrelevant; what is significant is the potency of this buried fear which appears to surface at the moment of mergence. There is an immediate disintegration afterwards in both *House* and *Persona*, which is not remedied for the remainder of book or film, with the possible exception of the ambiguous endings.

In *House*, the narrator spins off into her "madness" as a result of this fusion and the concomitant fears. In one of the most effective passages in the book, she describes the feelings which have arisen from this mergence:

> I am ill with the obstinacy of images, reflections in cracked mirrors. I am a woman with Siamese cat eyes smiling always behind my gravest words, mocking my own intensity. I smile because I listen to the OTHER and I believe the OTHER. I am a marionette pulled by unskilled fingers, pulled apart, inharmoniously dislocated; one arm dead, the other rhapsodizing in mid-air. (HI, 29-30)

The narrator's sense of self has been "dislocated" by this total mergence with her mirror-opposite. The image of her health and normality has been cracked, and she is left uncertain of who she is. She is divided between the reflection of herself which she presents to please the OTHERS and the buried shadow which has appeared as a result of this identification. Nin continues to depict woman divided against herself in unforgettable language:

> I see two women in me freakishly bound together, like circus twins. I see them tearing away from each other.

I can hear the tearing, the anger and love, passion and pity. When the act of dislocation suddenly ceases — or when I cease to be aware of the sound — then the silence is more terrible because there is nothing but insanity around me, the insanity of things pulling, pulling within oneself, the roots tearing at each other to grow separately, the strain to achieve unity. (HI, 30)

This is the nightmare of total duality: the desire for unity, intimacy, counterbalanced by the fear thereof; the outer woman, persona, at war with the shadow. The allusion to freakish circus twins suggests the spectral fear of "abnormality" which leads to conflict and anxiety. There is no distinguishing the "pulling within" and without; the outer "insanity of things" is incorporated within, the violence buried inside gets projected outwards. This is poetically stated here, and in *Persona,* dramatically demonstrated through a series of violent acts on the part of Alma towards Elizabeth, which mirror the cruelty of the outer world. Bergman also uses documentary evidence to make his point.

In the early part of the film, Elizabeth is in her hospital room and turns on the television, only to recoil in horror at a clip of a Buddhist monk immolating himself in protest against the Vietnam war. The camera focuses steadily on the monk; we are brought into Elizabeth's experience and feel the same horror that she feels. The "madness" of her silence throughout the film makes sense in the context of her revulsion from a world in which such violence regularly occurs.

Later in the film, we observe Elizabeth in one of her private moments in which she contemplates a photograph taken in the Warsaw ghetto, during the round-up of the Jews for the camps. The camera zeroes in on the pathetic figure of a little boy gazing in terror at the Nazis. The connection between private and societal breakdown is brilliantly revealed in this scene. Elizabeth's culpability in terms of her neglected child is suggested in her contemplation of the photograph.

Inner and outer nightmare converge for both Nin and Bergman but the latter has a greater apprehension of external, political nightmares, and the former, at least in *House*, remains trapped in the inner nightmare, reluctant to "pass through the tunnel which led from the house into the world on the other side of the walls" (HI, 70). This difference between the two is reflected in their imaginative conceptions of transparent images. The window in the house of incest, for example, looks out on a "static sea, where immobile fishes had been glued to painted backgrounds" (HI, 51-52). The window in the summer house in *Persona* looks out on the world, reflects back to the characters and the audience 'humans' capacity for cruelty to others. The fissure in the window occurs directly after Alma places the piece of broken glass in Elizabeth's path. Images overlap once again: fragments of broken glass appear in *House* as well, but in that case, the writer is cut by her own book, perhaps in punishment for the "labyrinth of selflove," the prison of narcissism: "As I move within my book I am cut by pointed glass and broken bottles. . ." (HI, 62). This image suggests the guilt and pain involved in creation, particularly when the life and art are inseparable. The book becomes a mirror of the artist and reflects back to her a shadow image. It is interesting that Nin conceives of the image in a rather masochistic manner, and Bergman in more sadistic terms. perhaps in keeping with social conditioning.

Although there is more inter-play between the world perceived through the window and the reflection in the mirror in *Persona* than in *House,* it is the private, self-reflective struggle with the "monster who sleeps at the bottom of . . . [man's] brain"[23] which predominates in both *Persona* and *House.* This struggle between the shadow-monster and persona is an on-going process without resolution in either work. This is what unsettles so many about book and film: there are no certitudes, and the conclusions about the possibilities of real change are tentative. Alma boards a bus at the end of the film, presumably to return to her old life, but whether she has been changed by the experience we can not be certain. We catch a glimpse of Elizabeth acting in *Electra* again but whether this is past or future is impossible to say.[24] There is the suggestion in this image of her willingness to resign the mask of her silence and to return to "ordinary" existence. The film concludes with the same exposure to the film process with which it opened; once again, the audience is forced into an awareness of the gap between life and art, and of the limitations of the artistic process.

No such reminder takes place at the end of *House* which, in comparison, is more affirmative. The book concludes with a woman dancing "with the music and with the rhythm of earth's circles; she turned with the earth turning, like a disk, turning all faces to light and to darkness evenly, dancing towards daylight" (HI, 72). Perhaps this is a movement towards acceptance of the light and dark sides of the self, of mask and shadow; or, put another way, a movement in the direction of the world outside the self, "towards daylight." Nin ends the book, as she began it, in process, moving towards completion of her "uncompleted self" (HI, 15).

NOTES

1. Anais Nin, *House of Incest* (Chicago: Swallow Press, 1958), p. 28. (Originally published in Paris: Siana Editions, 1936). Subsequent references in the text will be to HI.

2. It should be understood from the start that I am not implying a case of influences here. As far as I know, Bergman is unaware of Nin's book.

3. Oliver Evans, *Anais Nin* (Carbondale: Southern Illinois University Press, 1968), p. 26.

4. Stig Björkman, Manns, Sima. *Bergman on Bergman* (New York: Simon and Schuster, 1973), p. 198

5. Björkman, p. 168.

6. *The Diary of Anais Nin. Volume Two, 1934-1939* (New York: Harcourt Brace, 1967), p. 319.

7. Evans, p. 26.

8. John Simon, *Ingmar Bergman Directs* (New York: Harcourt Brace, 1972), p. 215.

9. Anais Nin, *The Novel of the Future* (New York: Macmillan, 1968), p. 119. Subsequent references to *Novel*.

10. *The Diary of Anais Nin. Volume One. 1931-1934* (New York: Harcourt Brace, 1966), p. 132.

11. *Novel*, p. 18.

12. Simon, p. 39.

13. Simon, p. 239.

14. Simon, p. 288.

15. Anais Nin, *In Favor of the Sensitive Man and Other Essays* (New York: Harcourt Brace, 1976), p. 116. Subsequent references to *In Favor.*

16. See Simon, p. 224; Björkman, p. 202.

17. C. G. Jung, *Two Essays on Analytical Psychology* (Cleveland: World Publishing Co., 1956), p. 203.

18. *The Diary of Anais Nin. Volume Four, 1944-1947* (New York: Harcourt Brace, 1971), p. 59.

19. *In Favor,* p. 112.

20. Anais Nin, *Seduction of the Minotaur* (Chicago: Swallow Press, 1961), p. 125.

21. *In Favor,* p. 114.

22. *Novel,* pp. 122-123.

23. *The Diary of Anais Nin, Volume Two,* p. 347.

24. Bergman claims that Elizabeth has returned to the theatre, but this is not clear in the film. See Simon, pp. 31-32.

The Art of Ragpicking
by Sharon Spencer

> There is no separation between my life and
> my craft, my work. The form of art is the
> form of art of my life, and my life is the form
> of the art. I refuse artificial patterns. Stories
> do not end. A point of view changes every
> moment. Reality changes. It is relative.
> *The Diary of Anais Nin, Volume IV*

Anais Nin is often imagined to have been a wealthy, expensively dressed woman, yet the truth is that many times she remade her clothes or wore dresses purchased from thrift shops. In the Diary she tells of transforming an inexpensive suit or dress into elegance simply by changing the buttons. Seemingly irrelevant, these examples of Nin's thrift actually point to one of her most characteristic attributes: the desire to go about collecting odds and ends; to restore meaning to what has been neglected and to give meaning to what has been ignored or derided. In short, Nin is a ragpicker of experience. And from the rags, debris, and especially from the broken fragments she has gathered up, Nin has made a large body of highly inventive books.

The essential motivation in Nin's life and art is a passionate desire to transform every thing, every experience, and every person, into a meaningful and valuable, if not actually a beautiful, entity. To use an unpretentious phrase, her art might be regarded as a vast reclamation project. To use a metaphysical term, it is an ongoing experiment in poetic alchemy. "Creation is an *alchemy*," she has written.[1] Alchemy is perhaps Nin's favorite metaphor for the process through which art transforms the ordinary into the extraordinary.[2]

Nin devoted her life to developing a poetic prose and to inventing structures that facilitated the transformation of her experience into

something precious. Precisely because, as she herself said, there is
"no separation" between her life and her work, because she succeeded in blending the form of her art with the form of her life and
because she rejects "artificial patterns,"[3] Nin inadvertently presents
a problem for traditionally oriented readers. They do not know *what*
she is writing: poetry; prose, memoirs; autobiography. Unable to fit
her books into historical literary categories, too many readers and
even critics dismiss them as inept. An essential aspect of the originality of Nin's books is that none of them fits traditional descriptions of literary genres. Her novels are more like sustained poems
than fiction. They are feats of improvisation in an imagistic prose
that renders character with psychological brilliance. Nin's Diary is
not a conventional diary, a spontaneous personal record, nor is it
fiction, even though the heightening of event and character, with
certain disguises of actual persons, brings this Diary intriguingly close
to autobiographical fiction. Anais Nin's literary criticism, too, re-
fuses categorization. Although her "unconventional" study of D. H.
Lawrence ignores the formalities of scholarship, it is a remarkable
achievement of impressionistic criticism and is still today one of the
most perceptive commentaries on Lawrence's writing. *The Novel
of the Future* is also difficult to categorize. Rich with comments
on novels and films that clearly detail Nin's convictions about writing,
this book flows beyond the boundaries announced by its title into
the realms of psychology, personal growth, aesthetic experience and
drugs, the nature of consciousness and of the self. It is a compendium
of all the themes that have absorbed Nin's attention since she began
writing. Anais Nin is not willfully misleading about her literary aims;
she is, though, a rigorously independent and self-committed writer
whose determination to express a private vision in literature links her
to the great moderns, particularly to Proust, and to the discoveries
in science and technology that were so richly suggestive for writers
during the first three decades of the century.

   Nin's assertion "I refuse artificial patterns" implies that for her
the "artificial" is that which already exists, having been brought into
being by someone else in order to fulfill someone else's expressive
needs. "Artificial patterns" are imposed by authorities, patriarchs,

priests, or critics who are committed to the protection and promotion of the traditional. In life and in art, Nin has rejected these figures of authority in order freely to create the patterns of feeling, thought, or expression that have seemed to her authentic when measured by a strictly personal intention.

Always rebelling, always improvising, inventing, struggling to translate everything she has experienced into creative work, Nin has, quite understandably, made the artist her hero. In this she echoes the Symbolists but especially Rimbaud's view of the artist as seer, prophet, *voyant*. She views art as one of the few meaningful activities of modern life. In this, as in much else, Nin is allied with Proust and countless other moderns who believe that, with the decline of the power of religion to sustain the sense of the mysterious, artists have inherited the powers that in previous ages were reserved for priests. These include the objectification of spirit in artistic forms; the task of providing man with inspiration to pursue his highest self; the redemption of the irrational; and the metamorphosis, through the alchemy of art, of the dross or base into a substance that is valuable and shimmering, golden, if not gold.

Nin's lifelong struggle has been the creation of herself as artist; this is the battle that is narrated in the published diaries. Her characters are usually artists. Besides Proust, the one wholly satisfactory, wholly admirable and always delightful person to appear in Nin's books is Jean (Janko) Varda who, in 1944, sent her a collage called "Women Reconstructing the World." The pages of *Diary IV* that describe Nin's visit to Varda in California are radiant. They crackle with the energy that Nin, discovering in the man, transformed into her description of him. Varda "concealed his sorrows." "He delivers us from the strangle hold of realism, the lack of passion and wit of other painters. He fulfills the main role of the artist, which is to transform ugliness into beauty." Above all, Varda "is in a state of grace with love and joy. He extracts from experience only the elixir of life, the aphrodisiac of desire."[4] The only female artist who is as fully self-possessed and as joyous as Varda is Renate, the painter. She appears in *Diary V* and in *Collages,* the experimental book of 1964 whose theme emerges from the presence of the artist, Varda

himself, in his magic role as the wizard who transforms ugliness into
beauty. When someone suggests that Varda make a portrait of Renate,
he declines, explaining that she is "'femme toute faite.'" Varda adds,
"'A woman artist makes her own patterns.'"[5] The very lack of pre-
existing themes and techniques leaves a woman artist entirely dependent on her personal resources; she is forced to invent the "feminine" for herself.

The fact that Varda is a collage-maker is extremely important.
Collage as a concept underlies Anais Nin's sense of art, both in theory
and as process. In fact, collage is, as Max Ernst has said, "visual alchemy."[6] The idea of collage is central to Nin's expression of the
modern spirit, so brilliantly prophesied by Guillaume Apollinaire in
1918 in his famed essay "The New Spirit and the Poets" ("L'Esprit
nouveau et les poëtes"). Here Apollinaire alluded to the electronic
inventions that would transform the twentieth-century arts. He
stressed the importance of the element of surprise as the "*greatest*
source of what is new," and presented a description of the collage
process. "There are a thousand natural combinations that have not yet
been composed. Men will invent them and put them to a good purpose, composing with nature that supreme art, which is life. These
new combinations — these new works of art — they are the art of
life."[7] Apollinaire saw that the new could be made from the old
simply by changing the types of elements brought into the composition, by using scraps of incomplete elements, or by combining familiar materials in unfamiliar ways.

Max Ernst and Louis Aragon, both of whom were connected alike
with Dada and Surrealism, have written of collage and both stress
the magic of this process. In *Challenge to Painting,* Aragon repeatedly
praises collage for its ability through "extraordinary displacement"
to achieve the realization of the miraculous (an aim of Surrealism).
For him collage is "black magic," for it leads the painter "toward
the magic practices which are the origin and justification of plastic
representation, forbidden by several religions." Ernst, the discoverer
of frottage, photomontage, and a brilliant exploiter of collage techniques, declares, "He who says collage, says the irrational."[8] For
the Surrealists collage possesses the power of transforming its compo-

nents into something altogether new and marvelous. Through "alchemy," dross elements are turned into a precious substance by the persistent art of the black magician, the prestidigitator, the Surrealist. There is a particular sense in which Anais Nin's art is related to the Surrealist ideal of magical creation through combinations of entities drawn from different categories. But her work is not itself Surreal, and it is easier to understand the application of the collage idea in terms of a broad definition. Collage includes all works in which components belonging to separate intellectual or peceptual categories are combined, regardless of the nature of the materials or the techniques used to combine them. Collage admits of endless variables. That is why Apollinaire was struck by its power to create the new. Moreover, the possibility of variety is extended because collage includes two types of materials: the ones collected for the composition and the means of fastening them together.[9]

The degree of novelty, shock, or surprise sparked by a collage will depend upon the degree of dissimilarity of its elements. The more "extraordinary the displacement," to quote Aragon again, the more shocking the effect on the audience. The more shocking, the more likely the work will be described as "Surreal." If the degree is relatively slight, the composition may merely seem somewhat offbeat or strange, intriguing the reader with a relatively small tremor of surprise.[10] The degree of displacement in Anais Nin's writing is relatively slight, even though there is considerable variety among her works. Her most experimental book, the one in which displacements are the greatest, is *Collages* itself. The early books, *House of Incest* and the pieces collected in *Under a Glass Bell,* display juxtaposition less in a structural sense than in stylistic combinations. Nin's diction is based on collage; she chooses words from a wide variety of sources and is usually successful in achieving a striking yet authentic image, phrase, or descriptive passage. A lover of words as words, Nin uses them if they appeal to her, regardless of standards of usage; she also draws upon far-flung vocabularies. "You can go into any number of sources. I draw from paintings, mobiles, scientific journals, dictionaries, films, plays, cities."[11] Guided by the unpredictable lure of free association, Nin combines into a novel the incidents that seem

most strikingly to project her characters' inner lives. In *The Novel of
the Future* Nin describes how she wrote *Collages*: "I allowed myself to
live out a mood and see what it would *construct* [italics mine]. Once
the mood is accepted, the mood makes the selection, the mood will
give fragments a unity, the mood will be the catalyzer. And so this
book, which should have been a novel or another book of short stories,
became something else, a collage."[12]

Like Anais Nin's fiction, her Diary is also a collage composition.
The assembled elements are the bits and pieces of her life: fragile
evocations of her feelings; her victories over herself; her occasional
moods of despair; richly detailed portraits of the people who moved
her, inviting friendship and compassionate analysis, or provoking her
disapproval and critical analysis; passages from books and letters;
passionate declarations of her aspirations as a writer; passages brilliantly describing the psychological problems of the artist; sharp observations of the cultural patterns of America; and fascinating accounts
of Nin's own repeated journeys into psychoanalysis. Selected from
the mass of materials of the unpublished diary, the passages that
comprise each published volume are themselves a collage composition
presenting a phase in the life of their creator.

Nin's Diary, a work of art in itself, possesses special importance
for those who are intrigued by the creative process. Because this
Diary exists, we can see exactly how Nin's fiction was made. Even
greater insights may someday be available to those who are able to
study the unedited manuscripts. But a comparison of the present
version of the Diary with the fiction reveals first, and perhaps most
strikingly, Anais Nin's insistent need to preserve her experience, the
stuff of her life, by recording it with astonishing dedication, even
passion. The intensity and power of this need explain why Henry
Miller and Otto Rank were unsuccessful in their attempts to free
Nin of the diary. The diary *was* her life, her inner life, which the
circumstances of her outer life prevented from receiving full expression. This need to preserve her experience, to protect it from
alteration, change, or loss, proves the depth and strength of Anais Nin's
creative will and inadvertently demonstrates one of the theories of
her most famous therapist, Otto Rank.

Rank is very convincing when he argues that the fear of death is an important characteristic of the creative or productive personality:

> There is . . . a double sort of fear: on the one hand the fear of life which aims at avoidance or postponement of death, and on the other the fear of death which underlies the desire for immortality. According to the compromise which men make between these two poles of fear . . . there will be various dynamic solutions of this conflict . . . For, in practice, both in the neurotic and in the productive type — the freely producing and the thwarted — all the forces are brought into play, though with varying accentuation and periodical balancing of values. In general, a strong preponderance of the fear of life will lead rather to neurotic repression, and the fear of death to production — that is, perpetuation in the work produced.

Anais Nin has insisted upon carrying out the project of the diary, one that not only embodies her life, but also possesses the very important potential for outlasting it. "The mistake," Rank wrote, "in all modern psychological biography lies in its attempt to 'explain' the artist's work by his experience, whereas creation can only be made understandable through the inner dynamism and its central problems. Then, too, the real artist regards his work as more important than the whole of life and experience, which are but a means of production — almost, indeed, a by-product of it."[13]

In Nin's case there is a special dimension of this creative drive that relates it specifically to collage composition: the desire to redeem experience. "'I stand for hours watching the river downtown. I look at the dead flowers floating, petals completely opened, the life sucked out of them, flowers without pistils. Punctured rubber dolls bobbing up and down like foetuses. Boxes full of wilted vegetables, bottles with broken tops. Dead cats. Corks. Bread that looks like entrails. These things haunt me. The debris. When I watch people it is as if at the same time I saw the discarded parts of themselves.[14] Characteristically, when Anais Nin visited a ragpickers' village on the outskirts of Paris, she found "touching" all the "mismated" and "un-mated" objects. Her response to this scene of poverty and devastation was to proclaim: "I could write here."[15]

"Ragtime," first published in 1938, is a dream piece, a symbolic enactment of the artist's reclamation project. Like Varda who says, "'I'm only looking for fragments, remnants which I can co-ordinate in a new way,'" Nin's ragpicker "never looked at anything that was whole.[16] His eyes sought the broken, the worn, the faded, the frag-mented. A complete object made him sad. What could one do with a complete object?"[17] As Rank has said, experience serves the cre-ator. A complete object may be a fine thing within its own frame of reference, but it is of no use to the artist.

As the dream of "Ragtime" progresses, the dreamer gradually be-comes identified with the ragpicker, who, of course, represents the artist. He wanders about a garbage dump packing his "swelling" (pregnant) bag with irresistible junk. The dreamer enters this land-scape as a passenger on the hump of a camel that is itself only the ragpicker's shadow. Later, as she strolls through a plateau of shacks, gypsy carts, and trash, the dreamer grows increasingly anxious be-cause of the squalor of the scene. "Inside the shacks rags. Rags for beds. Rags for chairs, Rags for tables. On the rags men, women, brats. Inside the women more brats. Fleas." The highly suggestible dreamer, imagining that she herself may come apart, explode into fragments, begins to clutch parts of her body to make sure she is intact. She stumbles upon discarded parts of her self. First an old dress, once a favorite. But the dreamer has grown, and when she puts on this dress, she can no longer "stay inside of it." Next she finds castoff parts of her body. A wisdom tooth. Her long hair. Naturally the dreamer is disturbed by the reappearance of these parts of her former self. Do they mean that it is impossible to get rid of the old self, to shed one's skin? "'Can't one throw anything away for-ever?'"[18]

The ragpicker answers this wistful question by leading his colony of vagabonds in the "serpentine song":

Nothing is lost but it changes
into the new string old string
in the new bag old bag
in the new pan old tin
in the new shoe old leather
in the new silk old hair
in the new hat old straw
in the new man the child
and the new not new
the new not new
the new not new[19]

With this reassuring lullaby in her ears, the dreamer falls asleep (in her own dream), only to be picked up along with other odds and ends of scrap and stashed away inside the ragpicker's bag (now suggestive, as well, of the sandman's pack). But the reader does not worry about the fate of this particular dreamer. He knows that she will be well used.

Collages, published in 1964, twenty-six years after "Ragtime," is a superb example of how an inventive writer can adapt a technique from the visual arts to literature, in this case fusing a variety of apparently unrelated materials into a striking composition. A more ambitious, a deeper book than its easy surface and gentle humor suggest, *Collages* is composed of nineteen short blocks of prose, beginning and ending with the same passage. This circular structure contains some twenty-two characters in an abundance of quickly sketched settings that range from Mexico to Europe and include California and New York City. *Collages* gives the impression of having been put together from Nin's writer's scrap bag, conceived from the energy of her determination to create something interesting out of her leftover characters, situations, and settings. Again, she wants to use everything. The cement that binds these colorful remnants is Renate, the painter whose portrait Varda did not want to attempt because of her completeness as a woman artist who "makes her own patterns." Renate is the strongest and the happiest of Anais Nin's women characters. She weaves in and out of the lives of the others, bringing silent inspiration. Renate is a dynamic example of the artist who sustains balanced relationships to her painting, to her friends, and to herself.

Although Renate dominates the design of *Collages,* her strong and bright area is balanced by Varda, with his tremendous energy and self-assurance. The portions that concern his life and his creations — so brilliantly evoked by Nin's descriptions — are exactly in the center of the book. And rightly so, for Varda's philosophy is the thematic core, teaching the need for beauty and how to achieve it by piecing together the splendid, life-enhancing visions that are called collages. Eventually, even Varda's rebellious teenage daughter succumbs to his spell. She gives up dirty jeans and sweatshirts in order to dress herself in "Varda's own rutilant colors."[20]

Collage art, like all art, works magic transformations. In this book Anaïs Nin repeatedly shows fantasy and dream enriching life, providing the loves that a narrow "reality" denies, dissolving the boundaries between the natural and the perverse, the impossible and the marvelous, comforting and reassuring the lonely and the isolated. There is an intense relationship between a girl and a raven. One character feels more akin to seals than to human beings, and he finally develops the courage to renounce people in order to be with the animals he loves. A gardener experiences delight by pretending to be a millionaire with funds to back a literary magazine. A woman who has lost her husband to a young girl replaces him with an exotic phantom lover, Shumla, a hero of Islam. In *Collages* imagination is sovereign.

The magic of intimate relationships balances the magic of art. *Collages* ends with the reluctant emergence of a woman writer from a bitter, self-imposed isolation. Judith Sands allows herself to be "courted" by Renate and an Israeli admirer, Dr. Mann. Much more relaxed and secure, opened by friendship, Judith Sands actually shows Renate and Dr. Mann one of her manuscripts. Its opening words are the same words with which *Collages* begins.

This repetition helps to endow *Collages* with its circular structure at the same time that it underscores Anaïs Nin's conviction that art is the "alchemical" magic through which life is redeemed. Our lives are ceaseless change, a never-ending process that moves from birth to maturity to decay and to the apparent death that is, in reality, a transformation of energy into a different form. Echoing the theme of the ragpickers' song are some wise words from the Koran that comfort the Consul's rejected wife: "'Nothing is ever finished.'"[21] Once an interaction of two persons has begun, especially if it is a lively one, it cannot be stopped but will continue to affect both from then on, however subtly and indirectly.

The elements Nin uses in her prose collages are drawn without exception from her personal experience. They are the people, the relationships, the situations, and settings she actually knows. To these she adds the knowledge arising from her interpretations of unconscious dramas, dreams, visions, and intuitions. She emphasizes the validity of unconscious experience, which she carefully evokes and analyzes. The vast tissue of Nin's entwined life and writings reveals the fascinating way in which the self mediates between conscious and unconscious experience, traveling between them like an artful spider, building an intricate structure from the relationships it creates in its ceaseless motion. Thus Nin's sensibility may be observed at work with the materials of her experience, busily shaping feelings, intuitions, observations, and ideas into the personal relationships that are always her subject matter. The fixative in her collage compositions is always a self in relationship. And from the presence of this self radiate perceptions and insights that endow the collage, whether it is a volume of the diary or a novel, with its particular design of feeling and form. In the Diaries and the books of criticism, the self that controls the design is Nin's own; in the fiction the author's self is concealed behind projections of other selves, characters based upon women with whom the author identifies in some significant way. In every case, though, it is the motion of this self toward awareness that provides the stuff that holds together the other elements in the composition of the book. The glue in Nin's collages is the "I" who perceives, reflects, interacts with others, dreams, interprets her experience, and, finally, expresses what she has experienced.

The concept of the self is very important in any exploration of Nin's writings, and it is difficult to isolate a single definition of "self," notwithstanding the many references to it. Nin does not seem to be concerned with the self as essence. Instead, she writes about the self in motion, in relationshiops with others, learning, searching, suffering, recovering, gathering still more experience. In short, Nin writes about the self as a process, almost as an urge toward the discovery and completion of itself. Gradually, though, it seems that Nin has come close to adopting a basically Jungian idea of the self. This influence began with the period of psychoanalysis with Dr. Martha Jaeger and has received more emphasis in recent years because of Nin's friendship with Dr. Ira Progoff. It is particularly important to distinguish between the self and the *persona,* the mask or socialized dimension of a human being. Nin's fictional characters are often trying to discover their selves and to separate their authentic desires from the confusion caused by overly powerful *personae.* The glossary included in Jung's autobiography, *Memories, Dreams, Reflections,* defines self as "not only the centre but also the whole circumference which embraces both conscious and unconscious; it is the centre of this totality, just as the ego is the centre of the conscious mind."[22] In "The Writer and the Symbols," Nin defined the supreme aspiration of her work: "The quest of the self through the intricate maze of modern confusion is the central theme of my work. But you cannot reach unity and integration without patiently experiencing first of all the turns of the labyrinth of falsities and delusions in which man has lost himself. And you cannot transcend the personal by avoiding it, but by confronting it and coming to terms with it."[23]

These confrontations and self-discoveries provide the subject matter of Nin's novels, as of her Diaries. Besides dream interpretation and the revelations of free association, she has explored the ways in which a self is affected by the selves of those with whom it is deeply involved. In *The Novel of the Future,* she wrote: "We know now that *we are composites in reality,* collages of our fathers and mothers, of what we read, of television influences and films, of friends and associates . . . ." Empowered by the act of perception, the self is a tool for connecting the conscious and unconscious realms. This is true of all people, but is much more obvious in the case of artists, whose completed work testifies to the success of the connections the self has accomplished. Since the self is individualized and each is unique, because of the varying elements of which each is composed, its way of seeing the world will necessarily be personal and, therefore, slightly different from that of any other individual. This is the source of the relativity to which Nin so often refers. Because each self has an individual vision, it is always in danger of distorting what it perceives. This is one more reason, in Nin's thought, why each individual needs to know his hidden self as deeply as possible, so as to discover his deficiencies in an attempt to correct his vision." The only objectivity we can reach is achieved, first of all, by an examination of our *self* as lens, as camera, as recorder, as mirror. Once we know its idiosyncracies, its areas of prejudice or blindness, we can proceed to relate with others. We cannot relate to others without a self."[24]

In dramatizing the journey of an "I" toward recognition of its self, again and again Nin chooses to explore the complexity of relationships or the impact of two selves on each other. She uses the terms "fusion" and "merging" to describe intense personal relationships.[25] Her characters, like her own self in her Diary, are always moving either toward an experience of fusion or struggling to become free from one. Nin seems to agree with D. H. Lawrence that this vacillation is natural and necessary. At times the self requires a state of fusion, and will be disappointed and even thrown into despair when it fails to achieve it. But at other times the self requires privacy, an opportunity to experience its own nature in solitude without the obligation to fulfill the demands of the other. "A man who lives unrelated to other human beings dies. But a man who lives unrelated to himself also dies."[26] The self, then, is obliged to live with instability; it is committed to a life of motion between its own boundaries and the personal territories of other people's psyches. Yet it is through this continuous change and adjustment of its perceptions that the self comes to discover it own nature. Through knowing others, we come to know ourselves and eventually the world. ". . . I could identify with characters unlike myself, enter their vision of the universe, and *in essence* achieve the truest objectivity of all, *which is to be able to see what the other sees, to feel what the other feels.*"[27]

The discovery of self becomes possible in the process of living relationships, of constant interaction between the individual and phenomena, the individual and other pepole. "Life is a process of *be-coming,* a combination of states we have to go through. Where people fail is that they wish to elect a state and remain in it. This is a kind of death."[28]   Our perceptions of reality depend upon the exper-iences absorbed by the self, and the self we are at any moment in time is partly dependent upon the kinds of relationships of fusion we have experienced and the ways in which they have affected our identities. Nin's basic view of self and its unpredictable journey though experience was already a part of her thought when she wrote her book on Lawrence. As time passed and she learned more about psy-chology, this idea became more detailed and more sophisticated, but her essential insight into the nature of fusion, the way in which one person seeks to fuse with another, was originally intuitive.

There are several possible motivations for the attempt to fuse one's identity with that of another person or persons. One of the most obvious is a sense of incompleteness or fragmentation. Fusion may complement one's sense of identity, as in intense friendship or ro-mantic love; the partners may be of the same or of opposite sexes. Merging, when it implies the submersion of a weaker in a stronger person's sense of identity, may have its origin in the same desire for a stronger sense of self but actually lead to a weakening of this identity when the personality of the stronger absorbs that of the more de-pendent person. These are negative examples of fusion or of merging. In Nin's early writing the dangers do, in fact, outweigh the psychic advantages of such close relationship. As Nin moves into maturity, however, this anxiety gradually begins to disappear. The fear of frag-mentation and loss of autonomy is slowly replaced by a confident reaching outward to enhance the self through a variety of identifica-tions and intimate assòciations. Nin's early prose works explore the terror of loss of self, either because of fear and inhibition, or because of a dependency that a weak person has disguised as infatuation or love. Paralysis of feeling, numbness, inability to experience emotion, as well as hypersensitivity, an uncontrolled capacity for empathy. can cause the self to split into seemingly unrelated parts. Variations on this theme are portrayed in *House of Incest,* in some of the stories printed in *Under a Glass Bell,* in "Stella" and "Winter of Artifice," and in *Ladders to Fire.*

House of Incest, Nin's earliest published "fiction," is an imagistic enactment in poetic prose of a woman's "perilous" journey. The "I" desperately longs to expand the dimensions of herself through fusion with two other women who dominate her dreams with relentless constancy and force. Inspired by Rimbaud's *Une Saison en Enfer*, *House of Incest* portrays the psychic torment of a woman who can experience love but not her physical nature. She cannot express sensuality or sexuality. The language of Nin's book evokes an oppressive atmosphere of erotic tantalization and paralysis; impossible pleasures beckon from every direction. The unnamed "I" is the center of the design. Her alternating yearnings to lose herself in one or the other of the book's phantom women give the composition its tension, the interplay of the "I" among her obsessive fantasies of Sabina and Jeanne, both of whom represent an unhealthy but intense relationship to eroticism. Inhibited, hypersensitive, paralyzed by neurotic conflict, the "I" is strongly attracted to the forms of fascination represented by these contrasting figures: toward the spontaneous, unthinking acting upon any sensuous desire, on the one hand; on the other, toward the alluring, forbidden, intense love of the brother, toward a sterile but safe love. In order to resist both modes of identification and resolution, the one infantile, the other perverse, the "I" must embark upon a journey into the House of Incest.

Like the "I" of *House of Incest,* the young woman at the center of "Winter of Artifice" seeks to expand her identity through an act of psychic fusion. The novella is a collage of relatively homogeneous elements that are held into design by the consciousness of the dominant — again unnamed — central personage. Again, too, a psychic adventure with fusion has a strong individual tone which gives the book its appropriate metaphors and rhythms. Projecting the love of daughter and father, Nin in "Winter of Artifice" evokes and interprets the ambivalence of fusion that she described in her book on Lawrence, defending this ambivalence as an essential factor in all relationships of deep involvement.

Again the reader is shown that fusion, though necessary to the ego of the developing self, poses serious risks to identity. One may be unwise in the choice of partner and find oneself lost, submerged, consumed by the other. This danger is the greater if it is a parent with whom one seeks to merge. The parent is usually stronger, and moreover is endowed with a seductive accumulation of experience, an air of authority and wisdom that feed the child's fantasy of being able to obtain anything, to heal any wound, by appealing to the all-powerful parent. Because of his original biological dependence, a child may easily lose his sense of self in the relationship with the mother. But the relationship with the father also presents a threat, particularly to the daughter Nin portrays; she suffers doubly from the expectations and needs of a child and those of a fantasizing lover. The daughter's yearning for fusion is intensified, as Nin explores this conflict in "Winter of Artifice," because of the twenty-year period during which she has been separated from her father. The daughter feels an almost irresistible pressure to hurl herself emotionally into the past to recapture this lost time.   Gradually, though, through intelligent analysis of her father's character, Nin's heroine is able to withstand the threat to her psychic autonomy. Her "womanly" way of conquering her vain father is to offer him an irresistible form of mothering. In an effort to avoid giving his love, the father cleverly chooses to regard his daughter as an "Amazon." Amazons, of course, do not need men. As long as the daughter collaborates in this perception of herself, she permits her father to continue to refuse all responsibility for her needs and desires.

Finally, the daughter confronts the reality of her father's selfishness. She strips away his "mask" (a frequent image) to disclose the manipulative and childish person beneath the elegant facade. "It was a struggle with shadows [when Jeanne kisses her brother in *House of Incest,* she is said to kiss a "shadow"] . . . . No one had ever merged with her father, yet they had thought a fusion could be realized through the likeness between them but the likeness itself seemed to create greater separations and confusions. There was a likeness and no understanding, likeness and no nearness."[29] In "Winter of Artifice" the desire for fusion is intense and even exciting, but it fails because of the threat it poses to the daughter's sense of identity, to her desire for personal liberty.

As she has repeatedly told her readers, Anais Nin's most valuable resource as an artist is her own complex self. Picking and choosing from the many and varied experiences of this self, she has created her ingenious books by combining elements that would not be found together in traditional fiction. She welds odds and ends of experience into collage compositions with the intensity of her personal vision of self and reality. As she has grown and changed, so have her books, reflecting the life that gave rise to them, just as the life has fed upon and been nourished by the books.

The quest that is traced again and again in Nin's writings actually involves a very radical concept: the abandonment of the idea of the self as a given fixed entity or essence. We create ourselves as we live, Nin explains poetically in her books and in the example of her own life that is revealed in the Diary. The idea of the self as a collage of experiences is central to Nin's psychological vision. Max Ernst, in writing of collage, quotes André Breton: "'Who knows if we are not somehow preparing ourselves to escape from the principle of identity?'"[30]

Such a question naturally provokes another: "escape" into *what*? Nin would no doubt share Breton's enthusiasm for escaping from the old-fashioned idea of identity as something fixed and given for all time, and she would welcome this escape as freeing people to meet the psychological challenges of the age of relativity, challenges which, from quite another perspective, were anticipated by Henri Bergson when he wrote *Creative Evolution*. The self is always engaged in the process of change, always modifying itself, altering, adapting, searching, expanding, growing ever closer to its most complete expression. Once again, relationship is the key to Nin's view of the self as a relativistic entity. "What happens is that two people [or three, or more] create a new alchemy. They interact upon each other and what takes place is not the leadership of one over the other, but the consequences of this interaction."[31] There are no limits to the powers of expansion of the self, not if the center is fortified. However, if the center has neither been accepted nor developed (and this is the case, for example, with Stella and Sabina), there is danger of fragmentation, disintegration, and destruction. Nin stresses the crucial difference between fragmentation and multiplicity: "rich personalities have many aspects but do not fall apart."[32]   In 1961 Nin was able to write with confidence: "The 'self' in my work is merely an instrument of awareness, the center of consciousness and experience, but it is like the self in Proust, a mirror for many other personalities, it is the core from which spring all kinds of relationships to others . . . . There is a constant, an organic preoccupation with development and growth."[33]

In Nin's life and art alike increasing complexity and increasing clarity have grown together as the self has passed from one experience and one relationship to another, always searching for meaning. Nin's desire for understanding has been enhanced by her artist's desire to "animate" knowledge, to give it the vitality and the unpredictability of life. "Relating one thing to another is almost what I would call a form of spontaneous life. The fusion of them is the alchemist's brew. I prefer my knowledge animated — that is, represented by a human being: a great doctor, an architect, or a painter. The living arts and humanities, caught in the moment of creating, talking, living."[34]

NOTES

1.   *Novel*, p. 40. Nin uses "alchemy" repeatedly to describe the power of art.

2.   Because Rimbaud's poetic doctrines and his attitudes toward dream and language have influenced Nin's writing, it is revealing to recall his prose poem "Alchimie du verbe." Nin continues Rimbaud's effort "to invent a poetic language accessible, one day or another, to all of the senses." This is why, as we shall see in the chapter on "symphonic writing," Nin has borrowed as many techniques as possible from painting, dance, and music. Wallace Fowlie, who has written extensively on French poetry and poets, has said of Rimbaud's poetic doctrine that it "seems to be a belief in the relationship which necessarily exists between a poem and witchcraft or magic or *sortilège*, as the French call it. A poem comes into being due to a process which, like alchemy, is magical and therefore foreign to the rules of logic and even the rules of instinct. According to this precept, a poem originates in this hidden life of the spirit and therefore is a reflection of this previous or submerged life." "Rimbaud: The Doctrine," *Age of Surrealism* (Bloomington: Indiana University Press, 1966 1st printing, 1950), p. 46.

3.   In *The Novel of the Future*, Nin explains "The process of crea-

tivity is this daring escape from conventional patterns, not because they are conventional but because they are dead, used up." p. 128.

4. *Diary IV*, p. 216, 217, 219.

5. *Collages*, pp. 70-71.

6. *Beyond Painting*, "What Is Collage?", an excerpt reprinted in *Surrealists on Art*, ed. Lucy R. Lippard (Englewood Cliffs, N.J.: Prentice-Hall, 1970), 126.

7. *Selected Writings of Guillaume Apollinaire*, ed. and tr. Roger Shattuck (New York: New Directions, 1948), p. 233. In 1918 Apollinaire had already written *The Cubist Painters* (*Les Peintres cubistes of 1912*), and he had observed the ingenious use made by Picasso and Braque of *papiers collés*, dating from 1912 when Picasso inserted a piece of oilcloth into a painting. The Cubists were to invent a variety of ways of varying the relationships of planes and surfaces by combining painted and pasted elements. Collage, however, has a history that stretches beyond modern art into twenlth-century Japan and to Persia of the thirteenth century. Collage includes the iconography of Russia and certain popular art forms like posters, ash trays, and paperweights (*kitsch*) made in the late nineteenth century in Europe. Before the twentieth century, however, collage forms were primarily decorative. Herta Wescher, author of a detailed study of collage, writes: "Not until the twentieth century, when creative artists took to working with it, did collage become a new and valid means of expression, one which has left its mark indelibly on the art of today," *Collage*, tr. Robert E. Wolf (New York: Harry N. Abrams, 1968), p. 19.

8. Louis Aragon, from *Challenge to Painting*, an excerpt reprinted in *Surrealists on Art*, p. 38; Ernst, p. 131.

9. There are many ways of fusing the elements of a collage besides pasting: for example, nailing; tying, sewing; welding; printing. In literature collage is created by juxtaposition. It may, as in the case of Apollinaire's own *Calligrammes of 1918*, involve the implementation of the spatial properties of the page with the words; or it may more simply depend upon combinations of writing which do not contain the traditional connectives (patterns of time, space, characters, incidents, themes, even transitions). In both methods the result will be that sense of novelty or surprise which Apollinaire and the Surrealists prized so highly as an effect of the "new" art.

10. In "The Art of Stillness," the essay which concludes his book *The Banquet Years*, Roger Shattuck distinguishes between heterogeneous and homogeneous modes of juxtaposition. Surrealist writing displays the former, and quite deliberately so, since it depends for its power of transformation upon violent contrast; so, too, does montage composition in film when it follows the ideal of its inventor, Serge Eisenstein. When the elements juxtaposed are more nearly homogeneous, however, the composition will give a calmer, a more serene impression, perhaps a sense of an underlying, if subtly patterned, unity.

11. *Novel,* p. 33.

12. *Novel,* p. 128.

13. "Life and Creation," *Art and Artist,* tr. from the German by Charles Francis Atkinson (New York: Agathon Press, 1968), pp. 47-48, 49-50.

14. *Diary II,* p. 106. Echoing Nin's ambitious project is Rosalyn Drexler's statement about a cross she sculpted from wood and rusty metal: "It was bought from my first show in 1960 and at the time, I couldn't believe that anyone else would want to own it. But I can understand it hanging in a church with all the gold and glitter and precious stained-glass windows. What has been discarded, used, thrown away is still holy — if not holier. I think art and religion are very close — the spirit of reclamation and love." "Dialogue," by Elaine de Kooning with Rosalyn Drexler, *Art and Sexual Politics,* eds. Thomas B. Hess and Elizabeth C. Baker (New York: Macmillan, 1973), p. 69.

15. "The Voice," *Winter,* p. 123.

16. "Ragtime," *Bell,* p. 58.

17. *Ibid.*

18. "Ragtime," *Bell,* pp. 59, 61.

19. "Ragtime," *Bell,* p. 62.

20. *Collages,* p. 69.

21. *Collages,* p. 91.

22. *Memories, Dreams, Reflections,* ed. Aniela Jaffe; tr. from the German by Richard and Clara Winston (New York: Random House, 1961), p. 397.

23. *The Writer and the Symbols,* p. 37.

24. *Novel,* pp. 84-85, 36.

25. Nin does not seem to distinguish between *fuse* and *merge.* In English, as in French, to fuse means "to unite or blend." But "to merge" is different because the joined parts do not remain equal; in a merger, one partner is *submerged* in the other. For a metaphysical approach to fusion, see Gaston Bachelard, *The Poetics of Reverie: Childhood, Language, and the Cosmos,* tr. from the French by Daniel Russell (Boston: Beacon Press, 1969: 1st French edition, 1960), pp. 197-198.

26. *Diary IV,* p. 154.

27. *Novel,* p. 68.

28. *Lawrence,* p. 20.

29. *Winter,* pp. 90-91.

30. *Surrealists on Art,* p. 127.

31. *Diary II,* p. 321.

32. *Diary IV,* p. 157.

33. *Diary VI,* p. 280.

34. *Novel,* p. 33.

The Song of the Womanly Soul: Mask and Revelation in Japanese Literature and in the Fiction of Anais Nin

by Catherine Broderick

'Put off that mask of burning gold
With emerald eyes.'
'O no, my dear, you make so bold
To find if hearts be wild and wise,
And yet not cold.'

'I would but find what's there to find,
Love or deceit.'
'It was the mask engaged your mind,
And after set your heart to beat,
Not what's behind.'

'But lest you are my enemy,
I must enquire.'
'O no, my dear, let all that be;
What matter, so there is but fire
In you, in me?'
                    —William Butler Yeats

Masks and masking are part of the human attempt to reconcile the world of appearances with the world of spirits, the ghostly world. The mask itself engages our mind as it does that of the speaker in Yeats's poem, for the mask promises a certain solidity and its fascination is akin to that of the witch's philter, the garden's apple, the Surrealists' fur-lined tea cup, the threatening pistol. The mind focuses on the object, held in thrall by the weight, not of the object alone, but also of its promise so terrible that reaching beyond the object to the promise is a formidable task. Yet there is always the shadowy knowledge that the mask holds not only the momentary safety contained in its solid contours, but something further, a revelation of what we in the twentieth century have come to believe is the "real," the "true." To transcend the surface reality bogging us down and to read the messages of the spirit world behind the masks is one of the liberating processes that literature offers us in our hopeful quest for the heart of our spiritual darkness.

From the revered Noh masks designated as National Treasures to the souvenir masks found in shops, the Japanese mask is both an aesthetic object and a common artifact. Its closest modern association is with the Noh drama in which, heavily influenced by Buddhist thought, the mask functions as a medium to show the process of fulfilling human destiny. In this cultural context salvation means working out one's destiny by cutting the ties that bind one spiritually and emotionally to the physical world before death and living at peace, resigned in the shadow of the mask that covers and defines one's fate. In the work of Anais Nin, to work out one's destiny means something different — it means to penetrate the irony of human duality and to see the mask as a two-sided object with the inner, revelatory side being the essential key to human fulfillment. Nin wishes to reconcile the conflicts arising from the struggle between the inner and the outer person through unveiling, unmasking. Resignation is the Oriental, reconciliation the Western way of dealing with the spirit world which is defined differently in both cultures; both resignation and reconciliation suggest philosophical and psychological value systems set up vis-a-vis the mask and its hold over forces we fear may swell beyond our control

Control over these personal forces, over the inner self, is a necessary virtue in Japanese culture as reflected in two constantly used Japanese words for self-expression: *honné* and *tatemae*. *Honné* is the true self, one's true intentions, motives, feelings, honestly-felt emotions. *Tatemae* is the mask, the pose one shows to the outside world, the inscrutable reserve one needs to deal with others. A Japanese expects to be treated to a display of *tatemae*; the mask is honored as a skillful as well as polite means of dealing with other people. *Tatemae* is not hypocrisy, as many Westerners erroneously believe, but a convention born from a recognition of the age-old necessity for reserve in dealing with others at constant close range. The narrow, crowded Japanese island life has created conditions which led to the necessity for internal barriers in social intercourse. The physical contours of the world do not provide such barriers for Japan. Successfully to conceal one's *honné* until the proper moment for revelation is a virtue for the Japanese, and because the *honné* may be hidden for long stretches of time, the mask itself comes to "engage the mind," "set the heart to beat" and serve as an object of aesthetic study. Indeed, Japan's mythological origins are in concealment rather than revelation. The Sun Goddess, Amaterasu-O-Mikami (Heaven Shining Great August Mother), hid herself in a cave. She had to be persuaded and finally tricked into revealing herself as the first ruler and, thus, ancestor of the emperors of Japan. Reluctant revelation and the primacy of the mask are fundamental to the concept of self-expression in the Oriental tradition.

In Anais Nin's fiction the Western tradition of revelation seen, for example in the Book of Revelations or God's revelation to Moses of the Ten Commandments, is inseparable from the concept that veils and masks are undesirable. The masks we prepare for outsiders, their destructive effect on the self, and the necessity of penetrating other people's masks as quickly and as thoroughly as possible, are fundamental tenets of Western psychoanalysis. Within Western religious and psychoanalytical traditions, Nin's novels and stories employ the ambiguities of masking as a principal theme. The definition and function of the mask as a barrier to essential and necessary truth, as the outer wall of a fort which must be surprised, forced or understood away to reveal the rich depths of the real person behind is that of the Westerner, Nin, who wrote in her *Diary*: "the whole obsession in my fiction is to uncover the disguises. I seek harmony. . . . In order to escape the world of the man . . . I disguised the woman in myself to be allowed to re-enter the world of the poet, the dreamer, the child. . . . The conflict in my life is the conflict in my novels: opposition of ugly reality to a marvelous intuition or dream of other worlds."[3] Nin's use of the mask in order to discover how to be rid of it is the antithesis of the Oriental use of the mask in order to maintain and protect the integrity of the self.

For the Japanese the mask functions as a truth-revealer, an oracle, the singer of the drama of the inner soul. It is not discarded even though its function may have been fulfilled. An example of this use of the mask appears in the work of the young Yukio Mishima, whose books Nin read and respected. His *Confessions of a Mask,* published in 1949 when he was twenty-four, is, on the one level, an account of "the removal of the protagonist-author's social mask, and an exposé of the real face hitherto hidden behind the mask." But, further exploring the function of Mishima's metaphor of the mask, we find that "if characters are masks through which [modern] authors 'confess,' then the homosexual protagonist of Mishima's novel is the author's mask which enabled him to confess. The mask was Mishima's means of fictionalizing his inner drama." Further, "the mask almost becomes a metaphor for the human condition. . . ." Mishima felt the paradox of "true" confession, "for only a mask with flesh can confess, and . . . he intended to write a perfect fictional work of confession. In order to pursue the ontological quest of the mask, a mask must be deliberately worn."[4] *Confessions of a Mask* , eerily evocative of Marcel Proust's *Remembrance of Things Past* both in theme and style, was Mishima's "confession" of his homosexuality and exposure of its roots in his childhood.[5] Sickly, raised as a semi-invalid by his grandmother, the young narrator one day found himself obliged "to act like a boy" at the home of his cousins. "The reluctant masquerade had begun," he wrote. "At about this time I was beginning to understand vaguely the mechanism of the fact that what people regarded as a pose on my part was actually an expression of my need to assert my true self which was a masquerade."[6] The young Mishima, faced with the need to break out of the confines of culturally defined masculinity, discovers and confesses his homosexuality with the restraint of a devotee of the mask — the intimate is revealed within the limits of the mask's contours, within his interpretation of the rules of the genre of the "I-novel," Japan's personal confessional novel in which the narrator-protagonist maintains the masked pose determined by the author. For Mishima, a controlled, non-self-indulgent analysis of human behavior served as an artistic mask for his real, but hidden, face. When the narrator of *Confessions of a Mask* talks about "the fierce, impossible desire of not wanting to be myself" (p. 199), he shows his attachment to the mask. Even when recounting his most lurid sexual fantasies, the author keeps the mask of the protagonist firmly in hand through the very words he uses as a screen for himself.

Nin's story "Hejda" is a thematically similar picture of a woman who desperately wishes to break out of the confinement of culturally defined gender. But Hejda is a mask-discarder, a veil-tearer who has no respect for the veil or the mask itself as a shaper of human experience. Hejda's retelling of her childhood lacks the control of Mishima's confession. Her exhibitionism is overblown, slack and embarrassing. By the end of the story Hejda has flung the mask, and its ability to shape experience, into a smooth surface with no loose ends, far away. Before this last chaotically revelatory unveiling, Hejda's self-expression was instinctively masked, limited to the psychological process of signal-sending: "The passageways that led one to Hejda were as tortuous and intricate as the passageways in the oriental cities in which the pursued women lost themselves, but all through the vanishing, turning streets the eyes continued to signal to strangers like prisoners waving out of windows."[7] Hejda's desire to be noticed, her hunger for something unknown, her signals, help in her own unmasking are revealed by her triple-sided plea: breaking the eggs inside pregnant hens, filling frogs with gasoline and causing them to explode, sadistically pumicing the skin of a friend — these are all actions of a girl who wishes to break through the mask, the veil covering her real self. But she does not know how and can only helplessly cry out for assistance through her actions. Mishima's sado-masochistic sexual fantasies of the bound and bleeding St. Sebastian are as repellent to most readers as are Hejda's sadistic actions, and as equally unconsciously produced — but Mishima goes on consciously to analyze his fantasies and their effects while Hejda remains unaware of the meaning of her display of inner desire. Mishima the mask-holder and Hejda the veil-tearer act differently in their respective pursuits of the same goal — liberation.

Even in love, Mishima's protagonist maintains his attachment to the mask; in his courtship of Sonoko he is both sincere and false:

> . . . my "act" has ended by becoming an integral part of my
> nature, I told myself. . . . To say it another way, I'm becom-
> ing the sort of person who can't believe in anything ex-
> cept the counterfeit. But if this is true, then my feelings of
> wanting to regard Sonoko's attraction for me as sheer coun-
> terfeit might be nothing but a mask to hide my true de-
> sire of believing myself genuinely in love with her (p. 153).

Hejda acts in the same "counterfeit" way, but neither understands
nor desires the mask as Mishima's protagonist does. When Molnar
watches her "repainting the black line on the edge of her eyes out
of a silver peacock," the sight "confounds him, ensorcells him" (p.
89). Like Mishima's protagonist, Hejda is seducing from behind a mask,
the mask of the beautiful odalisque. But unlike Mishima's hero, she
has no idea that her signal is the wrong one, that it does not correspond to her desire to be seen as an independent woman. Vis-à-vis
Molnar, the deceptive mask of the pliable, decorative Oriental woman
is unintentional, whereas Mishima's protagonist wonders whether
behind the mask "maybe I do really love her. . ." (p. 153). Without
skill in understanding the use of the mask, Hejda marries Molnar
without revealing herself to him; she wrongly assumes that he has
penetrated her veil and sees her as she would like to be seen. Her
unhappy marriage comes as a surprise to Hejda, for the veil she had
so heartily wished torn is the very fabric of Molnar's image of her.
The duality does not balance and Hejda is left alone, wildly attempt-
ing to hang on to her identity without a veil, without a mask. In
Nin's story we see no direction for Hejda's future after the veil's
destruction, but in Mishima's novel we see the road of the protagonist's future as clearly as the curves carved on the face of his mask.
   Hejda's tragic inability to meet Western expectations of personal
revelation, her total inability to cope with her much-desired unveiling
is dramatically shown in the story as the burden of the Oriental woman
who cannot function without her mask, who cannot imitate the Western liberated woman. In Japanese Buddhist tradition as seen in the
masked play of the Noh, woman's fate lies in the fact that love leaves
her with jealousies and resentments which tie her to the abyss between

yume ("dream") and *utsutsu* ("reality"), an abyss from which she struggles to be liberated into the realm where all is one.[8] This classic theme has been carried into the modern novel by Fumiko Enchi, who is often said to be Japan's finest woman novelist. In her novel of 1957, *Onnazaka* (translated as *The Waiting Years* in 1971), she tells the story of Tomo Shirakawa, who hides her *honné* of jealously and resentment under a mask of *tatemae;* Tomo masks herself as the pefectly obedient wife who finds agreeable maids to serve the household and to be the concubines of its master. The serene mask worn by Tomo Shirakawa is reminiscent of the masks worn by the actors who play the wives in the "woman play" cycle of the Noh repertoire. Like theirs, Tomo's mask reveals her true feeling about her husband in her shocking deathbed demand that her ashes be scattered rather than buried with his in the family vault. In Japan this is the ultimate insult to the bloodline of the husband. Tomo's final victory over him completes the circle of her struggle. As in the Noh, enlightenment arrives for the woman who has battled her passions and been tortured by them.

But it is in *Onna men*, of 1958 (literally, "Women's Masks"), that Fumiko Enchi develops most thoroughly the metaphor of women's veiled actions compared with the masks of the Noh "woman plays." Divided into three parts, each with the name of a Noh mask as a title to indicate an aspect of woman's character, *Masks* tells the story of a woman who is tormented by resentment after her husband's mistress, a maid in the house, trips her, causing the wife to miscarry. The wife's struggle to regain her own independent identity by repaying her husband's infidelity in secret, again by insulting his bloodline, results in her becoming a masked woman who manipulates others to achieve her revenge. But her revenge is her victory, and her skill in keeping her *honné* hidden until all is accomplished shows her woman's burden of sin, and her ability to endure much suffering as well as the mystery of femininity.

The Western psychoanalyst Otto Rank has explained woman's mysteriousness as being a willed or contrived invisibility: "Her real life is hidden, and she is hiding it!"[9] This concealment is not a virtue as it is for the Oriental woman; in what could be a gloss on Rank's words. Nin explains: "What was the mystery of woman. Only this obstinacy in concealing themselves — merely this persistence in creating mysteries, as if the exposure of her thoughts and feelings were gifts reserved for love and intimacy."[10] For Nin, woman must overcome obstinacy; she must learn to speak, to write, to express herself. The mystery is false and it must be transcended if woman is to fulfill herself. Nin's heroine Djuna expresses this: ". . . she had played a role of woman, and this had been the torment, she had been pretending to be a woman, and now she knew she had not been at ease in this role, and now with Paul she felt she was being transformed into a stature and substance nearer to her true state."[11] This is what Hejda had wished to find, the transcendence of the mask, the reconciliation of the spiritual, psychological forces behind it with the face she wanted to show to the world. The contrast with the Japanese heroine of Noh or of Fumiko Enchi's novels lies in the fact that in Japanese culture even revelation is quasi-secret. The heroine succeeds because of her power to endure the long masking, the long suppression of her true emotions. Nin's work represents a different value system, a heroine is expected to succeed in life through self-discovery and the revelation to others of her birth into her true self.

The jealousy and resentment which may keep a woman's soul from attaining enlightenment in the after-life of a Buddhist world are not so different from the manifestations of jealousy and resentment that kept Djuna in Nin's *The Four-Chambered Heart* from attaining peace or harmony in her life in this world. Indeed, the doll, washed up faceless at the end of the near-suicidal night on the river, is a mask, a discarded mask which speaks as eloquently as Hejda's roughly torn veil of the discarded persona of the "good girl," the doll-like woman who had ministered to the needs of others without first claiming her own identity. Unlike Tomo Shirakawa in Enchi's *The Waiting Years,* who maintained her masked state until the end of her life and achieved a revengeful victory rather than an awakening, Djuna reaches a sort of enlightenment of the self as the doll-mask is flung away and a newly harmonious view of life restores her to her own womanly soul. Unlike Hejda, Djuna can function as a whole person without the mask/veil, and can look forward to a future in which the mask will no longer be needed.

As we have seen, it is in the Japanese Noh/Buddhist tradition that woman's mystery is honored and described through the retained mask, and it is in this tradition that the ending of Enchi's novel, *Onna men* (*Masks*) shows the heroine, Mieko Togano's secret self revealed by the mask Fukai, which she receives as a gift from a Noh master. His daughter explains:

> "It's called Fukai, and the name can be written either of two ways: with the characters for 'deep well' or 'deep woman.' It's used in roles depicting middle-aged women, especially mothers. The Kanze school [of Noh performers] takes the name to mean a woman of 'exceedingly deep heart' — that is, someone mature not only in years, but also in experience and understanding. My father had his own interpretation, though. He liked to think of it as a metaphor comparing the heart of an older woman to the depths of a bottomless well — a well so deep that its water would seem totally without color."[12]

In the last scene of the novel Mieko kneels, looking at the Fukai mask which has come into her possession. "The pale yellowish cast of the mournful thin-cheeked mask in her hands was reflected on her face, the two countenances appearing faintly in the lingering daylight like twin blossoms on a single branch. The mask seemed to know all the intensity of her grief at the loss of Akio and Harumé [her twin son and daughter by her lover] — as well as the bitter woman's vengeance that she had planned so long, hiding it deep within her. . . ." (*Masks*, p. 141). As she studies the mask Mieko hears the cry of the baby she has waited for, the "official" grandson of the husband who betrayed her, the grandson and heir to the great family name; he does not bear one drop of Togano blood in his veins. He is the son of Mieko's retarded daughter, Harumé, who died giving him birth and who was herself the daughter of the lover Mieko had taken after the tragic miscarriage.

Even in her victory Mieko has not discarded her mask; on the contrary, she fully owns the "deep" mask she has worn, the Fukai mask which reveals her *honné*, and which she will keep. After all, only two or three people even know of her real intentions, and these intentions must remain necessarily masked, even in front of these two or three; her grandson must be unquestionably known as a Togano for Mieko's purpose to be truly achieved. Like Tomo Shirakawa, she will find her comfort in her secret laughter, but unlike Tomo, who sends her shocking death-bed request to her husband, Mieko does not even have the satisfaction of knowing that her dead husband can know of her victory. She is caught in "the heavy load of karma . . . helplessly laden with that unending and inescapable burden . . . a passion for revenge — an obsession that becomes an endless river of blood, flowing on from generation to generation" (*Masks,* pp. 126-127).

Fumiko Enchi is fascinated with the classic Japanese theme of the feminine obsession with jealousy, resentment, revenge, and an attachment to things of this world that can endure beyond the grave. In her novel the poses, the veiled actions symbolized by the mask reveal both the true self of the heroine and the true nature of woman. The three Noh masks Enchi uses as the three chapter headings in her novel are not meant as metaphors for individual characters, but as symbols for different aspects of woman's character itself. The qualities embodied in these masks are quite specific: Ryo no onna (literally, "spirit woman") "represents the vengeful spirit of an older woman tormented beyond the grave by unrequited love"; Masugami (showing the face of a young woman in a state of frenzy), portrays repressed sexuality, a state in which the cold contours of the mask conceal an attraction to violence; and Fukai is the mask of the "deep well," the deep woman. The masks portray types; the women, actresses who wear them in turn. Mieko, for example, is described as "a quiet mountain lake whose waters are rushing beneath the surface toward a waterfall." Hers is "the face on a Noh mask, wrapped in her own secrets," but she is clearly drawn as an individual masked woman rather than a representative of a specific mask. In Nin's novel, *The Four-Chambered Heart,* Djuna, like Tomo and Mieko, successfullly wears a mask of serenity in the face of Rango's cruel deceptions, but, because she lives in a culturally different context, she is not bound to an obsession for revenge, and her victory is over herself rather than others.

It is in Sabina, the protagonist of Nin's *A Spy in the House of Love*, that we can see a process of masking which is both intriguing and problematical when compared to the process of masking in the novels of Fumiko Enchi. Unlike Djuna, Sabina does involve others in her long masking as she pursues her obsessive search for identity. Sabina's mask takes many forms. When she tells of her experiences "everyone laughed at this which she does not consider humorous, [and] she laughed with them; and now it was as if all she had said had been written on a huge blackboard, and she took a sponge and effaced it all by a phrase which left in suspense who had been at the baths; or, perhaps, this was a story she had read, or heard at a bar; and, as soon as it was erased in the mind of her listeners, she began another. . . ."[15] Sabina, we are told, "was compelled by a confessional fever which forced her into lifting a corner of the veil, and then frightened her when anyone listened too attentively" (*Spy*, p. 10). Like Hejda, "at first she beckoned and lured one into her world; then, she blurred the passageways, confused all the images, as if to elude detection. (*Spy*, p. 10). Indeed, Sabina is similar to Mieko of whom it is said "she must be one of the last women who lives that way still — like the masks — with her deepest energies turned inward" (*Masks*, p. 26). However, unlike Mieko, the inheritor of the long Japanese tradition of women's "look of utter tranquillity" (*Masks*, p. 26), Sabina's first expression upon waking in the morning "was one of tension, which was not beauty" (*Spy*, p. 11). Her anxiety, the ill-fit of the mask, "gave to the face a wavering, tremulous vagueness, which was not beauty, like that of a drawing out of focus" (*Spy*, p. 11). Sabina is not tranquil wearing her mask; she is in a state of semi-terror because of it. Yet she clings to it, unable to discard it, unable to live in peace with it.

In contrast to Sabina's discomfort at appearing masked, the Noh performer, a man, masks himself readily as a woman and continues to speak normally in his man's voice, for the masked art of the Noh respects and maintains a duality, the duality of human experience with which the Japanese are comfortable. Sabina, a loving and spiritually faithful woman, masks herself as a female Don Juan and falsifies her voice to speak as such, out of a contrasting need to reject duality. Sabina cannot accept, cannot find the key to her inner unity as a person with many facets. Unlike the Noh, in which the masked imitation is not of exterior difference but of the inner core,[16] in Sabina, the "core . . . was temporarily supported by an artificial beam," for it was at the core "where she felt a constant unsureness, this structure always near collapse which could so easily be shattered by a harsh word, a slight, a criticism, which floundered before obstacles, was haunted by the image of catastrophe, by the same obsessional forebodings which she heard in Ravel's Waltz" (*Spy,* pp. 33, 35). For Sabina, the mask is illusion and she wears it uneasily. Unlike Mieko, for whom masking is partly a cultural expectation, for whom the real and the masked are not at war, Sabina's energies are turned inward, warring behind the mask she wears without a clear objective. The mask produces confusion which tosses her about with the indifference of an ocean storm.

Like Hejda, Mieko, Yasuko and Harumé, Sabina pursues her desire for fulfillment of her identity through her sexuality. But unlike their Japanese counterparts, who find the satisfaction they seek, Nin's women remain unsatisfied. Hejda finds no joy or delight with Molnar, only hunger. Sabina's "body will not melt, will not obey her fantasy of freedom" (*Spy,* p. 39). Because her "suspended desire," a symbol of her hunger for the unknown and for her ideal self, remains and "burns undimmed" within her, people mistake her passionate desire for self-fulfillment for sensuality. The ill-fitting mask that Sabina cannot discard becomes her burden as revenge becomes Mieko's. Sabina's unfocused view of her nebulous sense of self is transformed into an obsessive and neurotic dependence on the mask of sexuality. It almost seems as though she wears the mask to hide herself from herself; her sexual hunger is not a motivation for masking (as anger and bitterness are for Tomo and Mieko). When she leaves a lover in the early morning, "holding her cape tightly around her" (*Spy,* p. 62), she holds her cape (mask) frantically; she is still in conflict, still at a loss, still in need of the gift of another man, of Alan, her husband, who restores her identity to her and soothes the "painful tension of her nerves" (*Spy,* p. 62).

Turning from her sexual odyssey to the reassurance of Alan and his "unchanging room" (*Spy*, p. 17), Sabina feels that "if Alan repudiated her, it was the death of Sabina. Her existence in Alan's eyes was her only true existence" (*Spy*, p. 63). Sabina does not accept her personal responsibility to find her own identity, apart from her husband, as Mieko and Tomo were forced to do. The victory of these two Japanese women as unsung heroines of a personal war will not do for the Westerner, Sabina, who needs to understand the words which her friend Djuna speaks to her: "The enemy of love is never outside," says Djuna, "it's not a man or a woman, it's what we lack in ourselves" (*Spy*, p. 135). In her "fabricated" world Sabina only allows herself a series of one-dimensional masks; she allows herself to express only a single facet of her self at a time. She cannot see the possibility of unifying the diverse facets of her self and she is also unable to see the complexity of her partners: "Is it my fault," she complains, "if they only turned one of their faces toward me? (*Spy*, p. 136). The multidimensional self, the fully awakened self, the self true to its own core was Anais Nin's ideal. It eludes Sabina.

Sabina is at war with her mask; Mieko goes to war with the mask as her weapon. The Westerner's distrust of the mask is caused by the ideal of creating an individual self, independent of others, that can stand bared to the world. Unlike Tomo, Mieko and Mishima's masked protagonist, Sabina is betrayed by her mask; it frustrates her search for continuity and for identity. At the end of *A Spy in the House of Love*, the reader is uncertain of Sabina's specific fate but certain that she will not be able to achieve selfhood, fulfillment of happiness until she discards her mask.

At the end of *Masks* we are left with the image of Mieko

> kneeling on the floor in the slowly deepening dusk. She had lifted the mask Fukai from its box again, and was studying it in solitude. . . .
> The crying of the baby filled her ears.
> In that moment the mask dropped from her grasp as if struck down by an invisible hand. In a trance she reached out and covered the face on the mask with her hand, while her right arm, as if suddenly paralyzed, hung frozen, immobile, in space. (*Masks*, p. 141; the last words in the book)

At the end of Sabina's tale, she "slid to the floor and sat there with her head against the phonograph, with her wide skirt floating for one instant like an expiring parachute; and then deflated completely and died in the dust" (*Spy*, p. 139). Both Enchi and Nin conclude their novels with images of artistic transcendence. In Enchi's case it is the Noh mask, product of an ancient art based on the necessity of understanding the depths of the human soul and its subtle revelations in the cool contours of a wooden mask. In Nin's novel it is Beethoven's Quartets which "began to tell Sabina as Djuna could not, of what they both knew for certain: the continuity of existence and of the chain of summits, of elevations by which such continuity is reached" (*Spy*, p. 139).

The messages of the Noh mask and of Beethoven's music are similar. But the role of the mask itself differs. In the Oriental tradition one does not transcend the mask; rather, with the mask holding one's duality in balance, one transcends the chains of earthly karma to reach a higher understanding of self and humanity. In the Occidental tradition, as we see so fully developed in Nin's work, one must be liberated from the mask, from the conflict of the inner and outer, from dualism. To do this one reaches inward, to the masked unconscious where, as Nin wrote, in the "apparently chaotic world of the unconscious there is an inevitability as logical, as coherent, as final as any to be found in classical drama."[17] The reaching inward to transcend what the Westerner sees as the limits of the mask is, thus, not foreign to the internalized Oriental dependence on the mask for transcendence of everyday human motivations and moods. But, it is in the emphasis on the mask's role in revelation that we see the distance between the two. For Enchi, as for Mishima, the Japanese artistic emphasis on the mask as a function of self-discovery is quite different from Nin's emphasis on going deeply enough into the unmasked personal world to touch the sources of the self. Nin dramatically demonstrated this belief by her own actions: "I step on the stage of the Edison Theater," she wrote in 1972, "holding a metal mask before my face, sculpted by Suzanne Benton. I say to the audience, 'For centuries woman has worn a mask and played many roles. Today she is unmasking herself and showing her true face.'

And I removed the mask and read from the Diaries."[18] The explosive impact of woman's dropping of the mask and the revelation of woman's sense of self is as startling in Nin's Western writings as it is wrenching in Enchi's Oriental tales. The overwhelming achievement of both of these writers has been to show that, in spite of cultural differences, to dare to be honest in depicting heroines in crisis is to transcend limits of both self and art — it is to sing with a beautifully resonant voice the song of the womanly soul.

NOTES

1.   William Butler Yeats, "A Lyric from an Unpublished Play," *The Green Helmet and Other Poems* (Dundrum, Ireland: The Cuala Press, 1910; rpt. Shannon, Ireland: The Irish University Press, 1970), p. 8.

2.   Nyozekan Hasegawa, *The Japanese Character: A Cultural Profile,* trans. John Bester (Tokyo: Kodansha International Ltd., 1965. Originally published in Japanese, 1938, p. 38.

3.   Anais Nin, *The Diary of Anais Nin: Volume Four 1944-1947* (New York: Harcourt Brace Jovanovich, Inc., 1971), pp. 91, 92, 93.

4.   Noriko Mizuta Lippit, *Reality and Fiction in Modern Japanese Literature* (Whtie Plains, N.Y.: M. E. Sharpe, Inc., 1980), pp. 183, 187, 190.

5.   Mishima's similarity to Proust can be seen in such passages as: "One morning just after a snowfall I went to school very early. The evening before, a friend has telephoned saying there was going to be a snowfight the next morning. Being by nature given to wakefulness the night before any greatly anticipated event, I had no sooner opened my eyes too early the next morning than I set out for school, heedless of the time." (pp. 53-54)

Or: "Fanciful dreams of the journey to come, visions of its adventure, the mental picture of the somebody I would one day become in the world and of the lovely bride I had not yet seen, my hopes of fame — in those days all these things were neatly arranged in a trunk against the moment of my departure, exactly like a traveler's guidebooks, towel, toothbrush, and tooth paste. I found childish delight in war, and despite the presence of death and destruction all around me, there was no abatement of the daydream in which I believed myself beyond the reach of harm by any bullet. I even shuddered with a strange delight at the thought of my own death. I felt as though I owned the whole world. And little wonder, because at no time are we ever in such complete possession of a journey, down to its last nook and cranny, as when we are busy with preparations for it. After that, there remains only the journey itself, which is nothing but the process through which we lose our ownership of it. That is what makes travel so utterly fruitless." (p. 118)

Again: "Added to the gloomy irritation that always threatened me when I was alone, the grief that had so shaken the foundations of my existence this morning when I had seen Sonoko was now revived still more poignantly within my heart. It proclaimed that every word I had spoken and every act I had performed that day had been false: having discovered that it was less painful to decide a thing was false in its entirety than to torture myself with doubts as to which part might be true and which false, I had already become gradually familiar with this way of deliberately unmasking my falseness to myself." (p. 152)

And last: "Habit is a horrible thing. I repeated the kiss for which I had so repented. But this time it was like the kiss one gives his little sister. And by just this much did it savor all the more of immorality." (p. 198)

Indeed, towards the end of the book, to cover an awkward moment, the narrator's friend asks a third person, "You promised to lend me a book by Marcel Proust, remember? Is it interesting?" (p. 227)

6.   Yukio Mishima, *Confessions of a Mask,* trans. Meredith Weatherby (Norfolk, Connecticut: New Directions, 1958), p. 27. Subsequent references will be given in the text.

7.   Anais Nin, "Hejda," in *Under a Glass Bell and Other Stories* (Denver: The Swallow Press, Inc., 1948), p. 89.

8.   Granny Mountains: A Cycle of No Plays, trans. Royall Tyler (Ithaca, New York: China-Japan Program, Cornell University, 1978), p. 10.

9.   Otto Rank, *Beyond Psychology* (New York: Dover Publications, Inc., 1941), p. 251.

10.   Anais Nin, *Children of the Albatross* (Denver: The Swallow Press, 1959), p. 135.

11.   *Children,* p. 74.

12.   Fumiko Enchi, *Masks,* trans. Juliet Winters Carpenter (New York: Alfred A. Knopf, 1983), p. 138. Subsequent references in the text.

13.   An interpretation which emerged in a conversation with Juliet Winters Carpenter. I thank her for her insights shared with me.

14.   An interpretation which emerged in conversation with Juliet Winters Carpenter. I thank her for this and many other fruitful ideas.

15.   Anais Nin, *A Spy in the House of Love* (Chicago: The Swallow Press, Inc., 1959), p. 9. Subsequent references in the text.

16.   Nobuko Uenishi, "Getting to Know the Noh," *Mademoiselle,* November, 1967, p. 194. One of the finest explanations for the layperson of Noh, this article was, although unverified, probably written by Anais Nin's good freind. For Nin's meeting with Nobuko Uenishi see the *Diary,* Volume Six.

17.   Anais Nin, *On Writing* (Yonkers, N.Y.: The Alicat Bookshop, 1947), p. 27.

18.   Anais Nin, *The Diary of Anais Nin: Volume Seven 1966-1974* (New York: Harcourt Brace Jovanovich, 1980), p. 243.

"Let's Celebrate: A Memorial Tribute"
by Renate Druks

On the 5th of January, 1977, I went to visit Anais. A premonition that her physical presence was vanishing decided me to think positively, against all odds.

All the way to Anais's house, over Santa Monica, Harbor and Hollywood Freeways, I repeated to myself with an almost hypnotic beat: "Think positively! Think positively! Think positively!"

Anais was in bed when I arrived. She was concerned about me, as always, and wanted to know what I was doing, feeling and thinking. I wanted to hear her laugh, or at least see her smile. I clowningly told her about the latest absurdities in my life.

Suddenly Anais whispered something, barely audible. "Oh dear," I thought, "She is having a weak spell." I put my ear to her mouth, and she whispered again, secretively. No, this is not a weak spell. Anais wants to tell me a secret, I decided. I moved my ear even closer to her mouth and heard her whisper,

"Do you think I ought to prepare myself for death?"

"For whom?" I asked.

"For death!"

"Who's that? . . . Have we met? . . . I don't think I know him."

Anais smiled at my error.

I made the best of my mistake when I realized that the reference was not to a very important person I ought to know and I said:

"There is no such thing . . . It is an abstraction . . . we humans invented the word."

Anais nodded yes.

"And all this," I said gesturing, "is an illusion. The Vedantists call it Maya."

Anais nodded again.

We hugged and kissed and I left. But I turned around for one more look.

Anais still had a smile on her face. She startlingly resembed "L'incon-
nu de la Seine," the unknown woman of the river Seine. That same
haunting eternal beauty, that same peaceful sweet smile.

I would like to read Anais Nin's credo. A celebration of life.

Let's celebrate the refusal to despair —
Let's celebrate that there are so many willing to make the arduous
painful inner voyage through passionate expereince — in an effort
to recreate ourselves anew — and erase the programming we have been
subjected to —
Let's celebrate those willing to be jailed for their beliefs — willing to
lay down their lives against war —
Willing to defy false order and false laws —
Let's celebrate the crucial and determining moment in women's his-
tory —
when they are becoming aware of their gifts, power and strength —
Let's celebrate that we will no longer have children we cannot feed —
That we are fighting against war —
That we are fighting political hypocrisies —
Let's celebrate that we have heroes
And equally courageous women we have not yet recognized —
That women's contributions have now become visible —
Let's celebrate the individual struggle to create a world of freedom
beauty and love —
Let's celebrate those who run their own printing presses and publish
poems, those who paint the ugly walls of city buildings —
those who make underground films not blessed by Hollywood —
Let's celebrate the creative will —
Those who defy commercialism and possessions —
and write their novels quietly pursuing a work they love —
Those willing to live in houseboats —
Let's celebrate the gifts of individuals to the collective and a recognition that they are interdependent —
That we have fulfilled Jung's predictions, that a dialogue between
the conscious and the unconscious is vital to an integrated human
being —
Let's celebrate that we recognize the power of the dream to indicate
the turns on the labyrinth —

Let's celebrate that when I decided to share my inner journey with others, a deeper bond was made, deeper fraternities, deeper loves were discovered, and the response was that this was not my diary, but everyone's, ours. This is OUR diary they wrote, and we feel less lonely because we are all giving birth to each other.